One Rose Blooming

One Rose Blooming

Hard-Earned Lessons About Kids, Race, and Life in America

by Rose Martin

WITH DOUG TRUAX

CROFTON CREEK PRESS
SOUTH BOARDMAN, MICHIGAN

First Edition
10 9 8 7 6 5 4 3 2 1

Published by Crofton Creek Press
2303 Gregg Road SW
South Boardman, Michigan 49680
E-mail: croftoncreek@traverse.net

Book and cover design by Angela Saxon, Saxon Design Inc.,
Traverse City, Michigan
Cover photograph by Stephen Graham Photography,
Ann Arbor, Michigan

AUTHOR'S NOTE
The facts and events described in this book are true to the best of my
knowledge. Many names have been changed, however, to protect the
privacy of certain individuals.

Library of Congress Cataloging-in-Publication Data

Martin, Rose, 1942-
  One rose blooming : hard-earned lessons about kids, race, and life in
America / by Rose Martin, with Doug Truax.
      p. cm.
  ISBN 0-9700917-4-5 (alk. paper)
  1. Martin, Rose, 1942- 2. Women in charitable work--United States.
3. Parent and child--United States. 4. Interpersonal
communication--United States. 5. Race relations--United States. 6.
Proverty--United States. I. Title: Hard-earned lessons about kids, race,
and life in America. II. Truax, Doug, 1944-III. Title.
  HV541 .M385 2002
  361.3'092--dc21
                                        2002001640

This book is dedicated to the late
Willie James Simpson,
who always encouraged me to write.

"So many people walk around with a meaningless life. They seem half-asleep, even when they're busy doing things they think are important. This is because they're chasing the wrong things. The way you get meaning into your life is to devote yourself to loving others, devote yourself to your community around you, and devote yourself to creating something that gives you purpose and meaning."

Morrie Schwartz as quoted in
Tuesdays with Morrie by Mitch Albom

Acknowledgments

$\mathcal{I}$'D LIKE TO THANK Stan Mendenhall for his inspiration and support on this project; he is a guardian angel without whom this book never would have happened. My deepest appreciation to Judy Hanks for her constant help and encouragement on each and every venture I've embarked on for the last thirty years; Elizabeth Barlow for her unshaken love; Mary Watkins, whose smile will melt the hardest of hearts; and Martha and Robert Seward for their loving generosity.

I am grateful, as well, to Bill Haney, who served as Dutch uncle to this project from the outset and who also gave so generously and freely of his time and patience instructing me in the ways of publishing. And thanks to Jeff Mortimer for his careful and patient work in drawing out my stories and working on the early phases of this book. I'm grateful, also, to Doug Truax, who heard my voice and understood my message, and then helped me shape this book into what it is.

Contents

Foreword

ROSE MARTIN LIVES in a different world than
most of us. The physical place she voluntarily inhabits
is tormented by poverty, drug and alcohol abuse,
homelessness, and the lack of opportunity. It's a place
victimized by racial bigotry, and one where children
are vulnerable to a whole host of problems not of their
own making.

Most people know this same place—Ann Arbor,
Michigan—for its world-class University of Michigan
and for its highly educated, affluent, liberal, socially
active citizens.

Rose's spirit resides in a different world, as well.
In Rose's world, if there is a problem, you do something to solve it. If you see people who are homeless,
you find them shelter. If they are hungry, you feed
them. If they are discouraged, you give them hope. In

her world you listen to children — really listen — and you give your love unconditionally.

Anyone who meets Rose for the first time is quickly seduced by her presence, her intensity. Her throaty voice wells up from another dimension and can shake the truth out of the most deceitful soul. Her quick wit and charm draw you in, and you can't help but be impressed with her incredible memory for people, families, and events. She has the patience and dedication of a Mother Teresa, but her thoughts take shape in a language as colorful and raw as the streets she grew up on. Rose was "telling it like it is" long before the phrase was coined. She is a great storyteller; the words roll off her tongue — as a grandchild of hers said — like music from a choir.

And you realize that if she had any venal instincts, she could use her impressive talents to enrich herself personally. In truth, she has done the opposite. She lives humbly, and for the last thirty years she has been focused on her clients — helping them stay off drugs, stay on the job, or stay in school. She has also used her charm, charisma, and intelligence to convince the well-to-do members of the town to commit money and resources to help the less fortunate.

For Rose, there is no difference between her personal and professional life. She raised a wonderful, successful family — two biological children and six adopted children. As a social worker and community activist she brought aid and comfort to thousands of kids. Along the way she opened her house to over five hundred children (nearly all without compensation) many of whom stayed with her for three months or more. Five hundred!

I can testify to her hard work, long hours, and selfless motives. I have received calls from her at 11:30 at night while she was on her way to help someone and I was on my way to bed. I have heard her schedule meetings with clients in Detroit—a good hour's drive away—after 10:00 P.M.

Getting to know Rose can be unsettling for anyone comfortable in his or her life. Even those willing to contribute to the cause, especially those who like to attach strings to their contributions, may find Rose's hand on their shoulder, gently pushing them out of their comfort zone. Rose inspires people—black and white, rich and poor—to reach new levels of, as she would say, "spiritual maturity." She believes that money and wealth should not be accumulated but used to fix problems for people. This can be unnerving for those who measure their own worth by their financial portfolios.

She has not and does not aspire to material wealth. A review of the contents of her safe-deposit box and her often-mortgaged house are testimony to that. Rose simply counts her wealth in ways that do not occur to most of us—lives saved, friends she can count on, children whose lives will be better than those of their parents, the drug-free days of a client, people willing to volunteer to help someone else.

This book came about when Rose talked about a writing career. I thought she had a compelling story that should be heard by a wider audience, so I helped arrange getting her story in print.

One of my favorite stories about Rose's dedication to her calling took place as this book was being written. During the holidays of 2000, a man took his two children hostage in their house. He held the police of four municipalities at bay for three days. The man's ex-wife was a client of the Peace Neighborhood Center, where Rose had been director for nearly twenty-five years, and Rose had, through the years, provided a variety of services to the children who were being held.

There at the site of the standoff stood Rose — on the coldest day of the winter — with milk, juice, and Fruit Loops, trying to get some food to her "babies." When she wasn't on the front lines, she was caring for the half of the family that wasn't being held against their will.

In the middle of all of this, she was supposed to be finishing up the manuscript with an editor, but she called me from the front lines and explained that she couldn't meet the next day as planned because, she explained, "I am involved in a hostage situation." I had never heard that excuse before for missing a meeting. And who could argue with it.

Rose is a role model for many, to some almost a saint. But she is not without her detractors. Some chafe at her freewheeling style of getting things done. They find it outside the bounds of standard procedures and financial management.

Perhaps sometimes it is. But Rose is continually reaching beyond our safe and often ineffective way of doing things. She understands, as few do, just how great the needs of our community are. And because of the depth of her experience, she has unique ways of teaching us how to help people in need, how to communicate with our children, how to heal racial divides.

We live in an overly institutionalized society, where we too often feel content to leave the solutions of problems to this government program or that business institution—in short, to someone else. It's a world in which we grow cynical, detached.

Rose brings us a refreshing antidote to that cynicism—one we desperately need.

Stan Mendenhall
Ann Arbor, Michigan

ONE

As Straight As I Can

IF MY ADULT LIFE WERE A DIRECT RESULT of the way I'd been treated as a kid, I guess I might have grown up to be an ax murderer. Or maybe just a plain old drunk or junkie.

My mother died when I was seven, and after her death my four brothers and sisters and I lived pretty much on our own until the authorities found us; my father was seldom home because he had to hold down at least two jobs, and then he died when I was ten. By the time I was nineteen, I'd lived in thirty-eight foster homes. I was a weekend drunk by the age of eighteen and was all the way there by twenty. During my mid-twenties I was married to a man who beat the hell out of me time and again.

Yet I've had a charmed life. Why? Maybe because somewhere along the way, it occurred to me that the only way to live was to treat people like I *wish* people had treated me, not like they actually had. And when you've been abused, kicked around, and undervalued as much as I had been, you sure have plenty of time to think about how people should treat each other.

For thirty years I've been able to help other people, the last twenty-five of those years through a marvelous place called the Peace Neighborhood Center. The Center is a nonprofit organization that feeds hungry school kids, helps drug and alcohol users get sober, trains people for jobs, brings families together, sends needy kids to camp, provides emergency assistance of all kinds to families in crisis...just to name a few of our services. Nearly half of our programs are solely to help children.

We are not affiliated with any church or government organization, although some do help support us. Most of our money comes directly from private donations or the United Way.

In the twenty-five years I've been director of the Peace Neighborhood Center, it has changed dramatically, growing from a drop-in service to a multiservice agency where a client can get any referral on any service he or she needs. If we don't provide the service, we know where you can get it.

While we have carefully coordinated and supervised programs, we don't always do things by the book. Hell, I don't even know what's in the book. You certainly won't find it in the curriculum of the social-work programs at our universities. Our approach has been called unconventional, offbeat, and even—by a few critics—downright irresponsible. It's not. We just believe in getting the job done. Sometimes that involves the simplest of solutions. And sometimes it involves working on a problem till hell won't have it. We don't stop because it's five o'clock or because some regulations say we must.

My training for social work came on the mean streets and through the inspiration and guidance of people with the power to make the world a better place. Some of those mentors were the street whores who cared for me as a young girl; others were some of the best-educated, most cultured people you'd ever meet. What mattered to me was their passion to help, and the spirit in which they gave.

I've tried to live up to some of those role models in my life. I don't own much of anything. I've failed miserably in trying to start some businesses that would support services for the have-nots of the world. I work from morning to night to see that the job gets done. In short, I've given my life to helping people, and you know what? It's the easiest thing I've had to do in my life.

Maybe that's why people keep asking me how I do it. What philosophy drives me? Why haven't I been defeated through all these tribulations (although, God knows, I've been discouraged)?

Well, I hope this book helps answer those questions. I've known way too many people who could make a difference in the world if they just went the distance to help fulfill the needs of another human being. They have the best of intentions. They work hard. But they stop just short of committing themselves to help another person. They can't quite give their children the unconditional love they need. They can't quite share their wealth in meaningful ways. They get right to the gate, and they can't reach up and open it.

I can't help but think every day about the people I come in contact with who would be so much happier if they could just let go—if they'd stop glorying in sports and how much money they earn and start glorying in serving children, serving other people.

Wouldn't it be wonderful if, say, here in Ann Arbor where I live, we could get 110,000 people stomping and hollering—just like they do on football Saturdays at Michigan Stadium—because Jeremiah Johnson learned to read or because James Kennedy entered treatment that day?

Wouldn't it be wonderful if each of us would just reach a little deeper to help someone, to understand his or her true needs? Government programs, bureaucracies, public works—they all have their place. But ultimately it comes down to each of us making a commitment to do something meaningful for others.

Here's a little of what I've learned about helping kids, breaking down racial and income barriers, healing wounded souls, and bringing blacks and whites, haves and have-nots together. It may not be what they taught you in school; I sure never learned it there. And it may not be all that politically correct or said in the most polite terms. But it comes from my experience, and it comes from my heart. And I'm giving it to you as straight as I can.

　　　　　　　　ONE ROSE BLOOMING

TWO

Escape from the Ghetto

WHEN I FIRST ARRIVED IN ANN ARBOR in 1971, I noticed something strange. There was no trash in the streets, no stench of urine in the air. People I'd see running in the streets weren't escaping the cops — they were "jogging."

I was twenty-eight years old, born and raised in an East Coast ghetto, and I finally had my fill of getting the crap beat out of me for no good reason by my husband, Wayne. I had put up with it for eighteen months because I thought that was the natural way of things. One night as I lay in a hospital bed, a light went on in my bruised and bleeding head. Maybe in an ironic way my brute of a husband knocked some sense into me. Whatever. At that moment in a hospital in Camden, New Jersey, I knew that I couldn't live with a man who beat on me and still live with myself.

Making the decision to leave was the easy part. It

was no longer a question of whether I would leave. It was simply a matter of when I'd leave, how I could make it happen, and where I would go. Getting out, getting away, starting fresh with two small children, that was going to take some doing.

The first thing I had to do was figure out how to hide some money from Wayne. I'd need enough to buy tickets for my two babies and me. As for where I would go, Ann Arbor, Michigan, came to mind right away. Just a few days before, I had seen a job posting at the place I worked—A & G Foods—for a position in Ann Arbor. All I knew about the place was that it was in the Midwest somewhere, in that state shaped like a mitten, with all those big lakes surrounding it. Ann Arbor—I liked the sound of that name.

But if it wasn't Ann Arbor, it would be someplace else. Any place far enough away from the hellhole I was living in and a man who used any excuse—or no excuse whatsoever—to pound on me. Wayne would never admit it, but he resented that I was smarter than he was, and he felt threatened by my success at A & G Foods while his sassy mouth and sour ways got him fired or pushed around everywhere he worked.

I came home from work one day with good news to share with Wayne. We were always short of money and behind in payments. At last I had something to tell him that could change all that. One of the regional managers at A & G's Gino's Restaurant, I explained, wanted to promote me from working behind the counter to being a member of a four-man team that opened new stores for the chain. I stood there by the

ONE ROSE BLOOMING

kitchen table waiting for a "You go, gal," or some damn word of praise or congratulations. Something. Wayne just sat there, shaking his head. Then he got up, pushed me aside, and just walked out the door. He spent the night at a bar and never said the first word about it. Until two weeks later, when I gave him my paycheck.

"What the hell is this?" he shouted. He could see the check was for the most take-home pay either of us had ever gotten. The manager had doubled my pay from $35 a week on hourly to $72 on salary.

"How come they're paying you?" he seethed. "I'm the man; you're the woman. That's just how them honkies do, throw it in the black man's face, keep him down."

That was Wayne. If the sun didn't shine, Wayne knew it was the white man's plot.

Sometimes, with no notice or warning, he'd show up at my job, riled because I was the only black person there. "What you got in common with these white folks?" he'd say. "You don't know the things they going to do to you, girl? All you gotta do, look what their ancestors did."

If I spoke pleasantly to a Caucasian person on the street, as soon as Wayne and I got home, he'd be all over me with those fists. I knew better than to let him get me down on the floor where he could go at me with those roach-killer shoes he wore—shoes with toes sharp enough to kill a roach that has run up in the corner for safety, or to do some damage to a human head.

I was in and out of the emergency room all the time with black eyes, concussions, split lips, my ears all puffed out. Wayne would come and visit me and do me the big favor of pointing out just whose fault it was that I was lying there with a face like a hunk of raw beef. "If you didn't fight back, I wouldn't hurt you," he would say.

I'd just hold my tongue. Not because I was afraid he'd smack me again but because I'd be damned if I was going to give him the satisfaction of telling him the real reason I fought back. When I was whaling back on him in those fights, I was doing it because I had so much anger in me that it just had to pour out. If I hadn't fought back, I just know I would have exploded. I hit him back because it wasn't just Wayne, the brute of a husband, I was hitting. I was striking out against his bigoted attitudes about race and my children's exposure to it. I knew I couldn't beat Wayne—he was one tough ghetto man. But when we were done, he would damn well know he had been in a fight.

Long before I met Wayne, returning one blow for another was second nature to me. When I was growing up, I had lived for a while in a foster home with thirteen boys. Defending yourself was an accepted and respected rite of passage. I didn't know it then, but the knocks I took—and gave out—as a kid conditioned me for survival.

Our final battle was the worst of our marriage, not only for the brutality of the beating but for the circumstances leading up to it. Wayne had been up for a promotion as a machinist at work. It was a job he was well qualified for and should have gotten. He didn't. He ranted at me that he was passed over because he was black. Truth is, it didn't have a damn thing to do with his being black; it was because he was a hot-headed fool.

Still, I felt sorry for him. And I had an idea I thought might help.

"Wayne," I said, "you can probably still get that job."

I told him my plan, and he reluctantly went along with it. I invited his two white supervisors to our home for dinner. The evening went well, and four days later, Wayne came home with the news. He got his promotion. His bosses gave him the news but then they made a big mistake. They told him what a great cook I was, how fortunate he was to have a woman like me, and how a man with his talents and such a fine wife could do great things in that company.

Wayne gave me the headlines in a calm, even voice as I stood there smiling. And before I could say a word, he shook a fist at me and yelled, "Why would those motherfucking honkies listen to you and not to me? What did you say that I couldn't?"

I shouted right back at him. "What are you screaming about? You got the promotion. All we did was show them we have hopes and dreams and feel for our kids just like they do. Maybe they promoted you because once they came into your home and saw you as part of something normal, they could overlook that rough, crazy shit you do."

That's all it took. I ended up in the hospital. Wayne outdid himself this time. It took weeks for my eyes to open. Dr. Henry David, who patched me up and put me back together, warned me, "If you don't leave this man, he'll kill you. You cannot continue to take these beatings about your head and live."

That's when I made my decision to leave.

I got a part-time job at night in a dress shop. Every dime from my daytime job at A & G was used up in household expenses. But I gave the money from my night job to my Aunt Lu to save for a ticket out of this hell—a bus ticket, a train ticket, a plane ticket, anything that would get me and my young children, Kellyb and Joe, who were eight and seven at the time, a different life. A sense of hope.

I knew it was the right decision when I saw the effect Wayne's abuse was having on my kids—children born before I married Wayne. And that reality was seared into my mind dramatically one evening. Wayne was taking a bath when young Joe burst in on him and then Joe, apparently imitating something he had seen in the James Bond movie *Goldfinger*, grabbed a lamp and hurled it into the tub, hoping to put a shocking end to the man he'd seen beating his mother time and time again. Happily for Wayne, the cord was too short and pulled out of the wall before it hit the water. Wayne leapt out of the tub buck naked and started after Joe.

I jumped into the fray, grabbing Wayne's legs and trying to wrestle him down. But he was stomping and punching me to get free, and blood was flying everywhere. At least I gave Joe enough time to escape to the neighbors, although Wayne was so angry he charged right out on the porch without a stitch on. The next day he bought me our first color television to try and make up for the beating. My eyes were too swollen to see it for a week or two, and even after that I never could stand the sight of that television.

Wayne, of course, knew I was working a second job. He also knew that I was going to secondhand stores and bringing home suitcases and other items. Although this went on for five months, he was certain I wasn't going to leave.

"You ain't going to leave this house," he'd say. "Not with all the attention and support you get. Everybody's in love with you. You ain't going to leave this."

But I was. I even knew when. For about four months Wayne had been on a waiting list to receive hemorrhoid surgery. Finally, on a Monday night in May he received a call telling him he was scheduled for surgery the following Friday morning. When he checked into the hospital on Thursday night, I asked his doctors to please call me to come in just before his surgery because I had two small kids at home that I needed to look after in the meantime. I could be there in a hurry, I explained, since we lived only half a block from the hospital. Friday morning the hospital called and a nurse said, "Mrs. Langford, we're getting ready to give your husband a shot."

"I'll be right there," I lied. I hung up the phone and immediately called my brother Herb. "Stop by

Aunt Lu's house, get my money, and come get me and the kids. We're going to the airport."

"You're lying," Herb said.

"No," I told him. "Just hurry."

Being a good brother, he went to Aunt Lu's and retrieved the eighty bucks I had saved and then drove me to the Philadelphia airport. I put the cash on the counter.

"Where will this take me and my kids?" I asked the ticket agent. "One way."

He looked through the schedules and told me I could get to Detroit. Dang, I thought, that's near Ann Arbor.

"We'll take the tickets," I told him.

I arrived at Detroit Metro airport broke, with two babies and only the vaguest idea of where I was or what I would do next. But the relief I felt in finally escaping Wayne's grip overwhelmed any insecurity. I asked a man at the gate about shelters in Ann Arbor. He said they didn't have any there, that finding a shelter in Detroit would be more likely. I figured that would be more like the surroundings I was used to in Camden, so we arranged to take a shuttle into the city.

I wandered out on the streets of Detroit in hopes of finding a shelter. A cop was walking down the street ahead of us, and I thought he could direct us to a shelter, so I tapped him on the shoulder. He wheeled around, gun drawn and pointed right at me. I screamed in sheer terror. After he saw I was no threat, he eased the gun down and angrily asked why I touched him.

"I was trying to get your attention," I said, still shaken. "I'm looking for a shelter, but I don't want to stay here if cops pull guns like that. Where can a woman raise two kids and not have a gun pulled on her?"

"There's a little town thirty-six miles west of here called Ann Arbor," he said. There it was again — Ann Arbor. Shelter or no shelter, I decided that must be where we were destined to go.

The cop directed me to the bus station and I put down my last few dollars on a ticket for the three of us. By the time we got to Ann Arbor, it was Saturday morning. I walked directly to the legal aid office on Fourth Avenue with two questions for them: "Will you help me get a divorce?" and "Where can I live with two kids?"

The divorce would have to wait until I had six months' residency. As for a place to stay, they sent me to the Huron Tourist Home on Washtenaw Avenue since there was no homeless shelter. Now, I grew up in the ghetto and was left to fend for myself at the age of seven, but this tourist home was the damned craziest, most insane and drunken place I had ever lived. I was scared to death.

Every night I called my sister Doris collect to assure my family I was okay, although I often ended up in tears. After a week in this insane tourist home, I caught a break. My sister told me she had received a letter from Patty, one of the girls I had met when I was having Kellyb in the Florence Crittenden home for unwed mothers in Paterson, New·Jersey. Patty was living in Ypsilanti, Michigan, a small town just down the road from Ann Arbor. My family, afraid for my well-being, insisted I call her.

When I reached Patty on the phone, she was so happy to hear from me that she started screaming and hollering. "Get out of Huron Home and come stay with me and my husband," she insisted. Before long, her husband picked me up and I went to live with Patty and her family in Ypsilanti.

And what a relief that was. After living as a battered wife and mother in the New Jersey ghetto and then being thrown into the pandemonium of the tourist home, settling in with a real family felt like heaven. Here I had no enraged husband waiting to punch in my face, and the kids and I didn't have to dodge drunks stumbling through the halls. Life was looking a whole lot better.

Patty was a licensed practical nurse and she had two children. One of them, Tyler, had been born exactly one week after Kellyb at the Crittenden home. He suffered from asthma and allergies. Every so often he would go to the St. Joseph's Hospital to get shots that desensitized him and built up his immune system so he wouldn't stay sick and miss so much school.

During my first week with Patty, I accompanied her and Tyler to the hospital for the shots. While Tyler was in with the doctor getting the shots, Patty and I sat in the waiting room. She showed me a pattern for a dress she was making. She was a great seamstress.

After a bit, Patty cocked her trained nurse's ear as she heard a code come over the intercom. "Hmmm, somebody's in distress," she said. Then there was another message. "They sent for a crash cart," she commented as we continued to study the dress pattern.

People were running past the door. "This is a bad one," Patty said. "This is serious."

Suddenly Patty looked up to see her father standing in the doorway. He had been a much-loved janitor in the hospital for twenty-five years.

"Dad, what are you doing in here?" she said.

He just held out his arms.

"Dad, what's going on? What are you doing here, you big lug?" she insisted.

"Darling…" he started to say. Just then Tyler's doctor appeared behind her dad.

"We lost him," the doctor said.

"Lost who?" Patty said.

"Tyler," her dad said.

Tyler's reaction to the desensitizing medicine had been severe—and suddenly, tragically fatal. No one could believe it. Patty and her husband's family came from around the country for the funeral. It was an incredibly sad occasion. After the funeral, Patty's alcoholic mother, who'd been drinking most of the night before, came up to me when Patty wasn't around.

"Whore," she said, "get your ass out of here. Tell your story walking. We don't want your son here anyway. That's why my daughter's crying the way she's crying, because your son constantly reminds her of losing her son."

It was harsh, but I knew exactly how she felt. My son would be riding Tyler's bike and playing around the house. Patty's would not.

I didn't want to tell my friend that her momma had approached me like this. I just said, "Hey, me and my kids are gonna go back to Huron Tourist while all this is going on."

Patty, bless her heart, insisted I stay.

"We'll be fine," I said, and I took my kids and left. I had just enough money for the bus ride to Huron Tourist Home. When we got there, I told the woman at the desk that I needed a place to stay and handed her my wedding ring as payment.

"Ma'am," she said, " I'm not a pawn shop."

"I need a place now," I insisted.

She looked at my kids and me...and then at the wedding ring. "Okay," she said, "I'll hold your ring. That way I know you'll pay me."

I knew that I would pay her no matter what. But, I thought to myself, you're crazy if you think I want that wedding ring back. Little do you know how much pain it has caused me.

The ring bought me a few days' time, at best. I needed a job and a place to stay quick. I checked out the job at Gino's Restaurant. No luck there. The restaurant opening had been delayed.

After a week of beating the streets, I was getting desperate. I left the kids in the room by themselves with a lot of cakes and cookies to keep them from getting too hungry. I told them not to open the door for anybody. Then I went to the personnel office in Ann

Arbor City Hall. I arrived at 8:45 A.M. and waited for the personnel director. And I waited. And waited.

Finally, at ten minutes to five I got to talk with him. "Go down to the Department of Social Services and get food stamps and get yourself on welfare," he told me.

"I'm determined enough to sit in your office and bird-dog you all day for a job," I said, "and you're going to send me to welfare?"

I didn't come this far to be on any damn welfare, I thought.

"I'm too smart to be on welfare. I'll show you," I said. And I read a piece of paper upside down that was sitting on his desk.

Apparently he was impressed. Instead of sending me to the welfare office to get food stamps, he sent me to the Housing Commission. "They're looking for someone to work with tenants," he said. "You need a degree in social work for the job, but maybe they'll forgo it because you're so smart."

He called ahead and I went to this little office on Washington Street. It was the first of the month, which turned out to be their busiest time, and the office was in chaos. Even though they were scheduled to close at five o'clock, it was clear they'd be there for a while. People were running around frantically trying to take care of business. One thing led to another and before I knew it I was answering the phones. All I had to do was say "Ann Arbor Housing Commission" and ask whom they wanted to speak to. That wasn't hard. I worked there for an hour or more before anyone could see me. Don Johnson, the housing director at the time, finally came out and saw how I was running that front office and said, "You're hired; I don't care who you are."

I hurried back to the Huron Tourist Home and told the kids.

On November 8, 1971, I showed up for my first day of work as a tenant aide for the Ann Arbor Housing Commission. It was one of the happiest, proudest days of my life. I was hired through the Community Employment Training Act (CETA), a program to put folks who did not have a formal education into jobs where they could earn a living without welfare. On my first day of work they took my picture and then gave me a picture ID that said "City of Ann Arbor, City Hall; Ann Arbor, Michigan; Rose Martin, Housing Commission."

I held that card up and just stared at it. I'll never forget how good I felt. That plane ticket got me to Ann Arbor, but this was my ticket to a better life. Things would be different now. I wouldn't be a drunk. I would take care of my children. I'd feed them and pay the rent. I'd no longer have a man beating me down. And I had a job where I could use my imagination, where I could think.

I was twenty-nine years old, and I felt like I had finally found something that I belonged to.

My FATHER DIED WHEN *I* WAS TEN. *I don't remember him discussing race, but I do remember something he did when I was three or four years old.*

It was the dead of winter, about eight o'clock at night. And, man, was it cold. My mother was in the hospital having my baby sister, so my father was taking care of my brother, a sister, and me by himself.

There was a knock at the door. It was a white man. Don't ask me how the hell he managed to get on Liberty Street in Camden, New Jersey, without being killed. But there he was, and he was begging for food and a place to stay.

My father said he couldn't let him stay in the house with us because he had children, but he gave him food and half the tobacco in his tin and some cigarette paper and three blankets. My father told him he could sleep in his truck. My Uncle Norman, who lived across the street, was there and he was beside himself. Why would my father help out a white man, he wanted to know, when my father didn't have two nickels to rub together? When black men were being hung in the South? My father told him about Jesus posing as a beggar. "A hungry belly is a hungry belly. Hunger has no color," he said.

When my father got up the next morning, the white man was gone, but there were two pennies on the front seat of the truck.

THREE

To Have and Have Not

*W*HEN I WENT TO WORK FOR the Ann Arbor Housing Commission, I walked out of a world that for me had been 99.9 percent black and into one that was largely white. It was a culture shock you wouldn't believe.

People loved this town. To me it seemed so sterile, so uptight. But as a tenant aide, I was running a program that required people and money. Since I had neither, I had to go out into the affluent white community and solicit white people for money and for their commitment to the cause of the homeless.

One of the programs I started in 1972 for the Housing Commission I called Operation Education. Through it we enriched children's education by arranging trips to provide firsthand experience with the subjects they studied in school.

At one point, I was trying to raise enough money to take a group of kids to Washington, D.C., to complement their study of government and the Constitution. I went into one white lady's house to meet her and three or four of her wealthy women friends, hoping they would support the trip.

Entering the house, I saw a black maid who was pregnant. I stopped short; the flashback to the suburbs of Haddonfield and Cherry Hill, New Jersey, was just too intense. I had to leave the house.

I HAD BEEN MAKING FIVE DOLLARS a day and carfare working as a maid in the suburbs. Every day there were about thirty or forty of us black women who would catch a bus out of the ghetto and get off at a liquor store in Maple Shade where our ladies would pick us up and take us to their homes to work like dogs all day.

I'll never forget the day in September 1961 when this lady from Haddonfield picked me up. I was nineteen years old and seven-and-a-half months pregnant with my daughter, Kellyb. I was huge; Kellyb weighed nine pounds when she was born, so you know how big I was. I had just had some kind of growth taken out of the back of my head, so I also had a full head bandage. The woman I was to work for was only about twenty-five herself, and she was very petite, attractive, and had a husband—something I didn't have.

She put me to work doing windows. Well, there I was, reaching and stretching and climbing up and down this ladder as she sat there prim and proper having coffee and never once acknowledging that I'm as big as a house, although she did ask what had happened to my head.

After about forty-five minutes of this, she said to me, "I'm so glad you're here today, Rose." I just looked at her.

"I have such a good husband," she added.

Yeah, I thought to myself, turn the knife, bitch. I'm alone in the world and you're telling me all this shit.

But all I said to her was, "You're very blessed."

"Yes, I am. When I told my husband yesterday that I had missed my period and thought I might be pregnant, he called the employment office to get a girl to come do this work," she said.

And I was the girl. I looked her in the eye, came down that ladder, took my rag and dropped it in the bucket—at least I didn't throw it—and walked out the door.

She came running behind me screaming, "What's wrong? What did I say to offend you?"

Although I really needed her to take me back to the bus, I was bound and determined that I'd walk back to that bus by myself. Someone finally did take pity on me—pregnant and bandaged up as I was—and gave me a ride. But that was the last time I did day work.

IT ALL CAME RUSHING BACK, there in that beautiful garden outside this white woman's house in Ann Arbor. After a bit, the woman came out and asked if I was all right. I pretended I was just nervous because I needed their help so much and wanted to be able to communicate with them.

There were so many adjustments I had to make all at once in this white world. White people, I noticed, had a tendency to wrinkle up their foreheads when black people approached them. Clerks in stores, people at city hall—they started frowning, thinking, "What is this thing going to say to me?"

If you think I'm lying, go with me some day. It happens all the time. I brought this issue up to city council once during a discussion on some other race matters. The city council members told me it was because the town employed out-of-state white students from Alabama, Tennessee, and Kentucky who had grown up with racist attitudes. The folks on city council didn't want to see the problem among their own. But you've got to recognize a problem before you can do something about it. Once you see it for what it is, 70 percent of the battle is won.

Now people may not think it's important that some white people frown at black people. But imagine you're black and this happens to you all the time, in every facet of your life. Imagine that you're a kid and it happens to you when you get up in the morning, and when you leave the house, get on the bus, stop at a convenience store to get a cookie. Imagine that the teacher does it to you in the classroom. How are you going to feel at the end of the day? It may be difficult to articulate, but you'll feel miserable. And it piles up day after day after day.

But once we acknowledge the problem, it is also our obligation and responsibility to do something about it.

If I'm staring at you because you're a black man and I'm afraid you might hurt me, I need to do something about that. If one reason things aren't clicking for me is that my supervisor is white, then I've got a problem I need to take care of.

I got the greatest compliment from a very affluent white male one day. I was thanking him for something he had done for the community.

"I should be thanking you, Ms. Martin," he said.

"Why is that, Bill?" I wondered.

"Before I met you, I was very afraid of black people, particularly black men," he explained. "Now that I have known you and the people associated with you, I no longer have that fear. One of the reasons I hang in there with you is that it was a big problem in my life that has been resolved."

He went on to explain that he'd never had any personal experience with black folks to speak of. All he knew was what he heard or saw on TV.

"Did any black person ever hurt you?" I asked.

"No," he said. "It was just fear."

"Fear?" I repeated. "I'd be afraid if I'd had a negative experience with you, but I'm not afraid of stuff that I don't have a reason to be afraid of."

"Then," he said, "I'm like you now."

When I first came to Ann Arbor I wasn't having an easy time with black folks, either. I had a deep East Coast accent and everybody I talked with would say,

"You're from New York, aren't you?" That played a negative part in my being a tenant aide for low-income housing people. Who did this funny-talking bitch think she was, coming into the projects to tell them how to take care of their kids or how to live?

I wanted people to think I was from here, and I tried very hard to be a chameleon and blend in, but that accent would always give me away. It only worsened the fact that some black people already resented me, as black folks can do, because I had a little something on the ball.

But over the years I've also had plenty of black folks tell me that I not only taught them how to ride the horse of success, but I also taught them how to like white people.

One black man, Ed Gillespie, once said to me, "I'm fifty-three years old, Rose Martin, and I never gave a shit about no white man. When I was twenty, a white man and his wife pointed me out in a lineup and said I was the black man who had robbed their store. I went to Jackson State Prison for five and a half years. The guy who had actually done the robbery ended up coming to Jackson, too, and he said he was sorry I was in there, but he wasn't going to tell the story himself."

But Ed got over that resentment. "If you have taught me anything in the twelve years I've been associated with you, Rose—other than to be a good parent and not steal anymore—it's how to genuinely care about a white man."

Prejudice isn't just about color. I feel strongly that a lot of what black people call racism is arrogance on the part of white people. It is a superior attitude based on class and material wealth. It has nothing to do with race.

We are spiritually deprived, white and black. It's easier for us to understand a racial explanation for a problem than it is to explain a class thing. Everyone can rally around race. We can see that. We can see black. We can see white. But we can't see what I'd call spiritual immaturity.

Much of that lack of character has to do with control. Most people who have a lot become self-centered. They're focused on themselves and not on humankind. I believe we were born to serve humankind first, to serve each other. And I've learned that true spirituality can come from anywhere.

I had a client named Tom who was divorced and had custody of his kids on the weekends. He wanted his former wife to start bringing the kids to the police department in Ypsilanti every Friday to make the switch because when she came to his house she would create a scene and then report to the court that they were having problems.

I went down there with him to talk to the police about it, and they acted like it couldn't be done. They treated Tom like shit. Although he didn't even have to ask their permission to pick the kids up there, he was giving them the courtesy because I'd taught him to do things properly. Part of his pain and strife had been that he didn't obey the rules.

Well, the police were giving Tom and me a crock of shit, so I went to the phone and called about six wealthy, successful white men and told them I was at the police department. I told them I was catching hell and I needed some support.

Within half an hour, they started showing up. As they came through the doors, the police would say, "Sir, can I help you?" and these men would say, "I'm with Rose. She called me here to support her client."

Guess what? The police started treating Tom like he was the king of England. We had been there two hours trying to straighten this out, and all of a sudden the same officers who treated us like shit were licking our boots. You wouldn't believe they were the same people.

I turned to Tom.

"You see," I said, "that's why you can't fuck up. When you've got that kind of support, when you've got people who trust you, you've got to obey the rules. When you need help, this is the kind of help we get."

I said something else, too. "These people I called are the white people you hate — the ones you don't see. They left work and their lives to come here and assist you with this. Your hate is unfounded. It's something somebody has told you, or a way for you to feel good about being a failure because you have somebody to blame it on."

Tom walked around for months telling different people in his neighborhood what had happened and how he thought no white man would ever show up to support him with anything, let alone help him with his kids.

But that wasn't the whole story. A couple of days after we talked to the cops, one of those men called me.

"How does he do that on weekends?" he asked. "He pays child support for three kids, makes eight dollars an hour. How can he afford to take those kids on the weekend? It costs money."

I told the caller that on the weekends Tom usually tries to mow lawns in the summer and shovel sidewalks in the winter.

"Doesn't that take away from his time with the children?" the caller asked.

"Yes," I said, "but that's how he gets the money to feed them or take them to the movies."

"Those days are over," the man said. "Once a month, I'll give you a hundred bucks and you pass it on to him."

And that's what he did. I tried to put the money through the program so he could get a receipt and deduct the contribution for his corporation, but he refused. "This is coming from me personally," he said. "If this man is going to spend every weekend with three kids five years old and under, the least I can do is help by seeing he's freed up to be with them."

I get a lot of flak from black people in Ann Arbor for not going up against city hall any time an agency with a black director is under attack, regardless of the circumstances. You would think I'd put a Ku Klux Klan hood on. When three white men on my board came after me, everybody wanted me to say that it was a racial thing. The newspaper even wanted me to say it was racial.

I've spent twenty-five years trying to get people to rise above that, to understand that people are immature spiritually, that they haven't been taught how to care about other people. It's not always a racial thing. After all that time teaching these things, I couldn't come up and play the race card.

When my mother died, my brother Herbert E took care of us. There were five of us kids living in that house with no woman present. My dad was working about twenty hours a day. We weren't to tell anybody that there was no mother in the house. Herbert was twelve or thirteen years old, and he worked at the meat market taking people's groceries home.

For about half a year we were doing fine. The kids in my family have always taken care of each other, always been close. We had to be to survive. Then one day, I guess I was in the second grade, I went to school with no underwear on. I was jumping rope and the teacher saw it. Herbert E used to dress all of us and bathe us before we went to school every day. He would tell us to do certain things, and I had forgotten. Not wearing underwear was one of the worst things you could do. The teacher told the principal and the principal took me out of class and into the bathroom and grilled me. Then he took me home, and that's when he found out my mom had died.

My father reluctantly agreed to have us placed in an orphanage out in the country. After that it was a string of foster homes—I can remember the names of thirty-six of those foster parents, and I know there were two more I can't remember. In those days, the state kept you until you were twenty-one years old, so when I was eighteen and nineteen years old I was still being booted from foster home to foster home.

I never stayed anywhere very long. I had developed early. When I was ten I wore a 34C bra. Every one of those men but two thought I should be his sex toy. That's one of the reasons I moved a lot. I would be someplace for a few days or weeks and then I would run away or call my case worker and get moved because the man in that foster home had a hidden agenda.

There were only two homes where the man of the house didn't try to make any moves on me sexually. One was the home of Joe Moon. He was a huckster and he was very good to me. Joe Moon must have been about seventy years old and I was about fourteen or fifteen.

I used to go out on the truck with Joe Moon and sell his vegetables with him. But Mr. Moon couldn't count, and I would make change for him. He really liked me because I was young and smart and I always made him feel good about himself. His wife had been taking care of all his finances ever since they married, and they had been married about forty years. But after I taught Joe Moon how to count his money, he went home and started examining his financial situation. Well, Mrs. Moon didn't like that one bit because she'd been hiding and stealing his money.

Mrs. Moon called the Bureau of Social Services and told them I was a little fresh piss-tail girl, and I was sleeping with her husband. She told them to come and get me right away.

Most of the time, nobody gave a damn about me except my brothers and sisters. And nobody wanted a big kid. I had to withstand my case worker coming to me at least once a damn month telling me, "The reason I can't find you a place is because you're not little—you're not two, three, four, five years old." Sometimes I still wake up at night screaming *because even in my sleep today I can still hear that woman telling me that nobody wants a teenager. I know what it's like not to be wanted. Oh, I know what it's like not to be wanted.*

When I grew up, I asked Herbert E one day why he took such good care of us when we were little. He said, "Before Mom went to the hospital and didn't come back, she told me to take care of all you kids."

"That's funny," I told him. "Mom sat on my bed one night and said exactly the same thing to me." She must have been covering her bases.

FOUR

The Sweet Taste of Justice

ONE REASON I'M SOMETIMES ABLE to do things that other professional social workers can't is that I've lived through the same experiences my clients have. I don't have a formal education and a professional degree, but as they say, I've been there, done that.

When a homeless person stumbles into my office looking for help, I know how he or she feels because I've been homeless—more than once. When a drunk staggers in, I know what he's going through because I once drank heavily. When someone comes to talk to me about being divorced or a battered spouse, I understand that—and I have the emotional and physical scars to prove it.

Too often, young girls who are pregnant come to see me. I know what they're going through. I know how it feels to be scared and alone with a life growing inside you when you're only a child yourself. I was in a home for unwed mothers, and I was an orphan. When single parents come in, I understand because I spent years plodding down that road.

Only very rarely does someone come into my office and talk about something, like bulimia, that I haven't had firsthand experience with. So I understand when someone says, That's a stupid mistake I made and I want to fix it and get on with my life.

And that's why I could look at this mixed-up kid Joyce and see myself.

Joyce was eleven years old when she started going through Peace Neighborhood Center's programs. Her mother was a crack addict, so when Joyce was fourteen she came to stay in my home while her mother sought treatment. Her grandmother was also a heavy drug user. Joyce ended up living with me for about three years. When she first came to me she was doing very badly in school. I knew she could do better.

One day we were going over her report card, and I just threw up my hands. "Joyce," I said, "I don't know what I'm going to do. I don't know what I'm missing. Why do you get such bad grades?"

She knew I was irritated with her and she started crying. "I'm not going to tell you," she said. "I told my last foster mother and she said nothing could be done about it because it happened so long ago. And I told my grandmother and she said, 'Just forget it; you're going to get people in trouble.' And then when I told my momma, she said, 'You watch too much TV. You got this off television. You know I wouldn't let anything happen to you.' "

Joyce just sat there silent. She was working out in her head whether to tell me, how to tell me. I knew the best thing I could do was just keep my mouth shut. Minutes went by and we just sat there. I started to wonder if maybe I had figured her wrong. Then it all came pouring out.

Her mother and her aunt smoked crack cocaine heavily when Joyce lived with them in Miami, Florida. Joyce said the reason she wasn't doing well in school was that she had recurrent nightmares about what happened to her and her siblings and cousins while her mother and aunt were out smoking drugs. They would leave their children with a man while they were gone—sometimes for three or four days. Then this man would sexually abuse that entire family, the girls and the boys.

I hear these kinds of stories all the time, so I didn't get as upset about her sharing that with me as I did about the fact that the adults in her life told her nothing could be done about it. The more I thought about it, the more upset I became that the adults in Joyce's life said nothing could be done about this crime.

"So they said nothing can be done, huh?" I said to her. "Well, I taught you kids to be fair and to be just, and now we have to do something about this because this is someone that was unjust to you. When I teach you about doing the right thing, it doesn't mean people can do the wrong thing to you and get away with it."

Joyce's current foster mother, in my opinion, was one of the best foster mothers in the county. I've got a Ph.D. in foster homes, so I knew that this particular foster home was a great one. It was disheartening to me that this foster mother would tell Joyce that this hateful act had happened so long ago that nothing could be done about it.

So I went to a group called "Take Back the Night." These folks deal with the sexual abuse of women in Ann Arbor. I told them I had to hunt down a perpetrator and needed cash to do it. They gave me some money. But I needed more to carry out the plan I had in mind, so I also went to a couple of the people I can always count on.

There are five people in this city — I call them my guardian angels — that I go to in extreme cases to as-sist another human being. I can ask them for anything, small or large, and they have never turned me down. I've gone to some of them for twenty-five years. Sometimes I am so pushed and working so hard that I don't have time to justify to someone why I need the money. I don't want to spend three days to get them to understand why I'm going to do this. I can say to my guardian angels, "If you want to be part of something real good, let me have some bucks. All I can tell you is it isn't for me personally."

In Joyce's case, I went to these people, told them enough, and they came through. Then I went to two of our recovering male addicts — ex-cons who had turned their lives around and were doing well. I asked them if they would take time off from work and drive me to Florida. They said they would.

Next I called the Dade County Sheriff's Department and found a detective who heard me out. I asked him to find out what he could about this person who went by the name of Chubby Bristol. That name was all Joyce knew about the man.

With little to go on, the detective couldn't come up with any leads other than the address where Joyce and her mother used to live. So I said to him, "I guess if you can't find him, I'm going to have to come down there myself."

"That would be very expensive," he said.

"Maybe, but I'm coming. And I'll need you to back me up. Will you do that?"

"If you mean back you up like deputizing you, I can't do that. But if you mean back you up as in you find him and we'll come and get him, then yes."

I called the two recovering addicts who had agreed to drive me and told them the trip was a go. We picked up Joyce and three of her friends to keep her company and headed for Florida. As we drove through Ohio, Kentucky, Tennessee, and Georgia, I was thinking confidently how we'd find Chubby, kick his ass, and then drag him into the police department.

After we got to Miami, we checked into a cheap motel and went to the neighborhood where Joyce had lived. The two men with me were street people, and I was raised in an inner city, so we knew how to get around. But I had been living in Ann Arbor long enough that I felt uncomfortable out on the streets again. Brave as I had been while driving down to Florida, I hadn't thought about how this would reopen my own personal snake pit of a past. Here I was in Florida with people counting on me, and I was scared.

To pull off this kind of thing, you have to have a plan — a scam, really. And I had a good scam laid out. The way it went, I made out that I worked for an attorney's office up north and Chubby Bristol's great-aunt had died and named him in her will. I was the only one who could deal with Chubby, and there was a reward of $100 for anyone who could lead me to him. On those streets, with most people drinking and getting high, that was a real incentive.

We spent two days putting out that story. We would go back again and again to a little place where everybody hung out. Finally, a guy approached me. He was eyeing me like he didn't know if he could trust me. I knew how to get around that. I took five twenties from my wallet, folded them up, and tapped them against my hand while we talked.

This guy kept looking at me, then at those bills. Finally he said, "Okay, I guess you're straight. You can find Chubby Bristol where he works. He has a job over to the auto parts store on U.S. 1." It was too late to do anything that night, so the next morning I notified the detective I'd talked with earlier that I had Chubby in my sights so he should expect a call. I loaded up Joyce and the other girls and drove over to U.S. 1 looking for the auto parts store. When we found it, I went in alone and asked the first salesman I found if I could talk to Chubby Bristol.

"Chubby's not here right now," he said. "But he should be here any minute. He's due to start at eleven o'clock."

I went out to the parking lot and got back in the van and told my team we were getting close. At first, Joyce was excited, then she got real quiet, knowing she might soon see the man who had done terrible things to her. To keep Joyce from worrying, I told her that once this was over, we were going to stop for a day in Disney World. That got her laughing and joking for a few minutes. Then, with no warning, Joyce screamed.

"That's him!" And she pointed to a very large, middle-aged man getting out of a beat-up old sedan. I guessed him at six-feet-four and at least 250 pounds. He was dressed well enough to be behind the counter at an auto parts store, but he sure wasn't much to look at. He had a sullen look that seemed permanently painted on his face.

I hugged Joyce and told her everything was going to be all right, just quiet down and watch. The van had tinted windows so there was no chance of Chubby looking in. I told my ex-cons to get on the cell phone and contact the Dade County detective and tell him to get here as fast as he could. Then I got out of the van and caught up with Chubby before he got to the door of the store.

"Hey, Chubby Bristol. Man, I ain't seen you in a month of Sundays. Where you been?"

When you act real familiar with people who don't know you, they won't say they don't know you because they'd be embarrassed. I put my arm around Chubby's neck and hugged him. I was trying to buy time, hoping my men had gotten in touch with the detective.

I kept holding Chubby up, talking and being very suggestive and making like we had some history together. All the while, I'm saying to myself, "Where the hell is that detective?"

Chubby looked at me like he couldn't quite make up his mind. Was this someone he had met while high and had something with and just couldn't remember? Or was this some kind of con?

I kept moving in close, using suggestive body-language to mess up his mind. My scam was working like a charm. He was searching his dark and sinful past trying to figure out where he possibly might have met me. And he was warming up to the idea of this lady coming on to him.

Finally, after what seemed a lifetime in the presence of this child molester, the detective pulled up. Chubby looked at the police car, then back at me. He had the look of one mean old rat that had just seen the trap door slam shut. He was a bit dazed and confused as the detective questioned him. After all, he thought he'd long since escaped responsibility for molesting this innocent child. Then they loaded Chubby in the cruiser and took him away for further questioning.

When it was all over, I turned to the guy who'd made the call to the Sheriff's Department.

"Damn, Ed, what took that cop so long to get here? I thought I was going to have to get in bed with Chubby right here on the street."

"Well," Ed started to say, "I...I...I...ca...ca... called..."

Would you believe it? I forgot Ed stuttered, and in the excitement of the moment it took him forever to get the word to the detective. Ed was a good man, just the guy we needed for the job. And he gave a lot of support to the kids during this ordeal. I just should have realized we'd need a little more time for the deal to go down.

We went to the Sheriff's Department, where they interviewed Joyce for hours about the abuse she had suffered. Eventually Chubby was convicted and went to jail, although the charges were watered down and he didn't get nearly what he deserved.

But the important thing was that Joyce was released from her imprisonment. Her nightmares stopped. Her marks went from Fs and Ds to Bs and Cs. She even got an A in one course. She stopped fighting with classmates and stopped disrupting teachers. Joyce was a terrific kid prior to this. Afterward she was even better.

I got some satisfaction in knowing that Chubby served some time, although I'd have been happy to throw away the key once they locked him up. But that wasn't why I got up in arms and drove across the country and stuck my neck out in those tough Miami neighborhoods.

I did it not only because that bastard Chubby had hurt this child, but also because the adults in Joyce's life refused to recognize it and do anything about her pain. Joyce had the courage to tell her foster parents, her mother, and her grandmother what horrible things had been done to her, and they just wanted to sweep it all under the rug.

You can't ignore that kind of pain. You can't gloss it over. Joyce needed to experience justice — to know that people cared about what happened to her and that people would not tolerate others not treating her well.

What are the chances of most poor, underprivileged kids being vindicated and receiving some small measure of justice? I'm afraid in most places they are about as good as being offered a scholarship to Harvard.

But at least one child got to sample the sweet taste of justice.

TURKEY SHOOT

AFTER MY FATHER DIED, *my brothers and sisters and I were sent to live on a small farm near Indian Mills, New Jersey, a little town east of Camden. The farm was the home of Douglas and Amanda Reed. They had no children of their own and we were the first group of kids they took in.*

The Reeds were one of the few black families in Indian Mills, and they were respected members of the community. Mr. Reed raised crops and farm animals, and he usually had about eighty turkeys on the farm.

During the fall Mr. Reed would hold turkey shoots to raise additional money. Every Sunday, he'd put up thirty or thirty-five targets and men would come from all over to see if they could win a turkey by shooting closest to the bull's-eye. Mr. Reed would collect fifty cents or a dollar from each of them, which would amount to maybe fifteen or sixteen dollars for the day, which was a lot more than the turkey was worth.

Mr. Reed would take me out every damn day during the summer when school was out and he'd have me shoot a rifle for hours to practice hitting that bull's-eye. Then he went and got a shotgun and I had to spend hours practicing with that gun, too. When other kids were out playing, I'd be out there in the woods shooting those guns.

Each fall when the men would assemble for the Sunday turkey shoot, what they didn't know was that the little twelve-year-old girl—me—had been practicing her butt off and could hit that bull's-eye nearly every time. Those men would go ape shit. "How can that little girl shoot like that?" they'd say.

But if Mr. Reed started the day with eighty turkeys, he nearly always ended it with eighty turkeys because I'd take home the prize. And you darn well know I didn't get anything out of it.

One day Mr. Reed brought a hair-trigger gun out in the field for me to practice with. And he kept saying, "Don't forget, it's got a hair trigger." My brother Ted was with me and when he went out to remove the target that I had used up, I bumped into the gun just a little—I didn't touch the trigger or anything—and the gun fired on its own, sending a bullet downrange.

By the grace of Almighty God, the bullet missed my brother. But I was shaking like popple trees in the wind and Douglas Reed was shouting, "I told you it had a hair trigger!"

"I don't want to touch it no more," I told him right then and there. "I don't want to touch it no more."

"You going to touch it," he yelled back. "He's all right. Boy, you all right?"

Just the thought that I could have hurt my brother Ted messed me up. I vowed to never pick up a gun again—and I sure never did while I was at the Reeds—although I got a beating for it.

FIVE

Guardian Angel

I WAS WORKING ALONE at the Peace Neighborhood Center the day before Thanksgiving. There was a huge amount to get done before I could deliver food baskets to needy families.

The phone rang. On the other end was a teenaged boy we'll call Jason. He wanted to kill himself.

Now, I was fairly new to the Peace Neighborhood Center. I started working there in April 1976, five years after I arrived in Ann Arbor. And I certainly didn't have any training in this sort of thing. To tell you the truth, I was scared to death. And to make things even scarier, five minutes into the conversation, Jason fired a gun to show me he meant business.

In those days we didn't have cordless phones, so while I continued to talk with Jason I had to carry this huge phone base with me as I packed the Thanksgiving baskets that had to be delivered. I didn't want to disconnect and lose this kid.

First, I suggested he call the teen suicide prevention hot line. But that made him angry. His friends at Pioneer High School had told him that I was the one who could bring some normalcy to his otherwise abnormal life.

I looked at all the baskets that needed to be filled for poor people. I looked around the room and noted that the place was empty, which was odd since somebody was always coming or going at the Peace Neighborhood Center—twenty-four hours a day it seemed. It was clear that spiritually he was mine. I had to deal with this on my own.

Jason told me he was from a very wealthy family. He was sixteen years old and felt he couldn't communicate with his parents. He said his parents liked money more than they liked him. He could not make one decision on his own, he said. His momma purchased his clothes and brought them to him. His dad was only concerned with whether they fit him or not.

To make matters worse, he liked a girl who was from a very poor family, and his parents wanted to control his seeing her. He had questions he wanted to talk to his parents about, but he could never get their attention. They were always in a hurry to catch planes, sign contracts, plan receptions, and make more money. They were always busy doing those things wealthy people do to stay wealthy.

Things came to a crisis for him when he took the car out without permission and had a fender-bender. He knew they would take the time to deal with him about *that*, and he was going to kill himself before they got home.

Jason and I talked for three or four hours as I balanced listening and packing baskets.

"Look," I finally said, "I have twenty-two baskets here to deliver to needy families. Why don't you help me? It's getting late. I will talk to you. I will stay with you as long as you feel you need me. But I have to deliver these baskets now, and I could use some help."

He was silent.

And then I said, "I will talk to your dad."

"You will?" he said. "My dad doesn't like black people. He's a racist."

"I will talk to your father," I assured him.

"Even after I told you that he's a racist?"

"C'mon, help me deliver these baskets, and we'll go and talk to your dad," I said.

"Okay," he said. "It will be worth postponing my death to see how my dad interacts with you."

I picked him up in the van in front of the old post office at Main and Catherine streets. He learned a lot in the next three hours as we delivered baskets. He saw kids at home without parents. He saw kids living in incredible poverty. At one home there were roaches running out of the baby's bassinet, and the baby's bottle was covered with fungus. At another house he talked with kids who had a foreclosure sign posted on their door.

As promised, when we were done, we went to his house in an entirely different part of town.

"Dad, dad, someone's here to see you," he screamed as we entered.

"Who the hell is it this time of night?" his dad yelled back. "I'm not expecting anyone."

"It's your guardian angel," I hollered back.

When he turned the corner with an incredulous look on his face, I gave him a very warm and loving smile. I could see that the first thing that shot into his head was, "I don't want her to know I'm prejudiced, but what's this nigger doing in my house?"

I introduced myself. He had read about my work in the community in the paper, and he had also read the "Rose Knows" columns that I wrote weekly for kids and parents. That legitimized me a bit, but you could see he was still uncomfortable.

I said to Jason, "Why don't you get yourself something to eat and let me talk to your dad?" He left the room obediently.

His mother came in and looked appalled. I had on blue jeans and a sweatshirt, and I was very sweaty from the day's work and the deliveries. But nonetheless I sat down on this beautiful melon-colored sofa. The chair next to it was darker, and I could have sat on it and not risked staining it. But I thought I would look good on that sofa.

As I sat down and spread out on the sofa, Jason's mom and dad looked at me like I'd kicked them in the shins.

"As I said, I'm your guardian angel," I said calmly. "Your son called me today. He says he wants to commit suicide."

His mom grabbed her throat.

"Yes, suicide," I said, "and to assure me he wasn't kidding, he fired a weapon. I could hear it go off over the phone."

His mother clutched her throat a little tighter.

"Aren't you lucky," I told them. "Aren't you blessed today. Because someone has given you an opportunity to make right whatever your son feels is wrong."

I explained to them in detail what their son had said to me and why he felt that he didn't want to be on earth any more. At that point his dad wanted to call him into the room.

"No, this is a conversation between you, your wife, and your guardian angel," I told him.

After a while, I could see them relax and start to appreciate that I had come. Whatever prejudice they had was rapidly disappearing as our hearts met. I told them about being a parent with eight natural and adopted children and how I loved them all. I told them I felt about my children just like they did about theirs. And I told them, too, that I would have been devastated if a stranger had brought me the news I was bringing them, but how absolutely blessed they were to be hearing it before a catastrophe happened.

I was careful not to condemn them or say they had caused it. And I could tell they appreciated that.

"What's good about your situation is you got a two-minute warning," I said. "These are early indicators telling you that you are walking on dangerous ground. You know the Negro spiritual, 'My Soul

Looks Back and Wonders'? Your soul says to you, 'I wouldn't do that.' The caution flag goes up." Well, chances are pretty good they had never heard that Negro spiritual. But they followed my drift.

Jason's dad told me how he didn't have much growing up. He wanted more for his son.

"We all want the best for our children," I said. "I know because I want more for mine. But you have to set boundaries—on yourself," I told him. "Wanting more for your children and earning more so they can have an easier lifestyle shouldn't take the place of your time to live with them. You could work less and spend more time with your child and still have a great life."

After a while Jason's dad sank down on that melon-colored sofa alongside of me. "Ms. Martin," he said, "where do I go from here?"

"I'm not the one to tell you," I said, "but I know someone who can. We need to get in first thing after Thanksgiving and see that person."

By that time, Jason had joined us.

"Do you want to spend the night with me or stay here with these guys?" I asked.

"I'll stay with these guys," he said.

"Do you want me to sleep here?"

"I think I'll be all right, Rose."

"I made a new friend today," I said. "But I'm an orphan, and I have abandonment issues. I get upset when my friends are not around, so be here when I get here in the morning."

I gave him my home phone number and told him I'd sleep with the phone next to my bed.

"Call me, meatball, if you need to talk to somebody," I said. "God has been very good to me; I don't require a lot of sleep, so don't worry about bothering me. Oh, and one final thing, Jason. Why don't you let me take that gun?" He hesitated, but went to his room and brought it back to me. I handed it to his father.

When I left the house that night, Jason hugged me. I thought he would never turn me loose.

"I thought you said your dad didn't like blacks," I said.

"You're different," he said. "He likes you because you're different."

I looked at him and said, "Not really. It's just that I had a trump card when I went in that gave me enough leverage to touch him, to help him change himself."

"What was that?" he asked.

"You."

That started a wonderful friendship between Jason's family and me. They were able to save their family and change themselves. It was a struggle, but at least they were able to do it because they were willing to change. Dad had to be gently reminded on many occasions what not to do again because he would gravitate to what got his family in trouble in the first place.

But Jason's dad did what many of us won't do — he accepted positive change.

"You have a way of saying things to people so they accept it," Jason's dad told me later. "I didn't feel rejected. I didn't feel you were blaming me. Not many people come into your home and tell somebody what you told us and leave so much comfort and joy."

"That's because we didn't bullshit each other," I said to him. "The people who taught me how to provide services also taught me that I have to meet people where they are with their understanding. I'm a parent; you're a parent. Your kid told me he had some problems, so let's not go anyplace else except where we can meet. Let's talk about parenting. Let's talk about sons."

The next week we had more than a dozen affluent white kids who came to the Peace Neighborhood Center wanting to talk about this or that problem or wanting somebody to help them. That was a lot of white kids to have there at one time. The kids from the projects were used to seeing these kids only in a school setting. I was delighted. Why? Because kids should be able to get what they need regardless of income.

One kid was seventeen and wanted to get married. He said he could handle it and go to college later. Another boy was despondent because the boys in his gym class had told him he wouldn't be able to satisfy a girl because his penis was too small.

Later I had a young girl who was contemplating suicide because every one of her friends had befriended her because of her money. She couldn't find a genuine friend until she met some kids in the South Maple housing project.

The easiest thing I ever had to do was tell the truth to kids, regardless of their means. Kids understand so much more than we give them credit for. If you are mature enough to explain it to them — and face their demons with them — kids can handle it.

And you can learn a great deal from kids if you're willing to be open with them and share with them. They can tell you all kinds of things that will be helpful to both of you.

The only time they won't communicate is when you haven't told them the whole truth, when you've held back. Kids will give you a strange look when they know a piece is missing. They haven't been on the planet long enough to know what's missing, but they know something is.

Just like Jason did.

ESCAPE

THE REEDS WEREN'T USED TO HAVING KIDS *in their home when all six of us came to stay with them. Amanda Reed would spend a lot of time with us, and her husband would get jealous because he was no longer the center of attention. They'd argue a lot, but it never came to blows.*

Then one Sunday night he went out with his boozing buddies and he came home drunk and belligerent. He and Amanda got into a horrible fight—we could hear it going on downstairs from the little unfinished loft we slept in—and suddenly he grabbed his shotgun and started for the stairs yelling, "I'm going to kill them."

Amanda Reed was a fraction of the size of her husband. She wasn't five feet tall and didn't weigh over 110 pounds; he was at least six-foot-three and weighed some 260 pounds. But she jumped in front of that big-ass man and fought him at the bottom of the steps, trying to prevent him from getting to us.

As we peeked over the banister we could see blood flying everywhere as he beat her with the butt of that gun.

"We got to get out of here," I told my brothers and sisters. We scrambled to the only window in the loft and climbed out on an old wooden fire escape that was covered with grapevines. We fell into bushes at the bottom and got all scraped up. I grabbed my youngest sister, Doris, and we all started running for the gravel road, scared as we'd ever been.

We kept running down that road in the pitch black, feet bloody and hearts pounding. I remembered it was right along here that just a few weeks earlier I had come upon the first dead person I'd ever seen; he was lying face up near the gravel pit. I'd seen bodies in the funeral home before, but I'd never seen anyone in the street lying dead.

We got past the gravel pit and a car stopped and picked us up. The driver took us to the state police barracks and we told them what had happened. But no matter what we said to them they were determined to take us back to the Reeds, and that's just what they did.

Mr. Reed, as I've said, was well thought of—no one knew what was going on in that house. He answered the door calmly—there was no sign of Mrs. Reed; for all we knew she could have been dead—and he did his little Mr. Charlie thing with the white police. He was talking with them like they were brothers, which made our story go down the drain. The police told him we were found out on the road. And they never asked to see Mrs. Reed.

"What are you kids doing out?" Mr. Reed asked us, and then turning to the white officers, he offered, "Kids do the darnedest things, don't they."

As soon as the police left, we shot up the stairs that were all covered with blood, shut ourselves in, and all piled into the same bed that night.

The next morning when we got up to go to school, Amanda Reed was in the kitchen. Her eyes were all big and jet-black and closed. I mean that man tore her up.

"Do you love me?" she asked.

"Yeah, momma, we love you."

"Then don't tell a soul," she said.

And we got on that school bus and went to school with that ugly secret trapped inside us.

SIX

Getting Real with Kids

$\mathcal{E}$VERY PERSON SHOULD LEARN MORE about being a good parent. We take parenting skills too much for granted. We treat them as some God-given talent that doesn't have to be learned. And as a result, too many parents — rich and poor — do a lousy job of raising their kids.

People with children at home aren't the only ones who need to acquire these skills. Most of us have nieces and nephews, grandchildren, children in the neighborhood, or others who need adults in their lives who understand how to interact with kids.

There's plenty of loose talk these days about family values and the importance of the family in our society. But there is far less discussion of what those values are and how we can improve upon them. We need to take a fearless moral inventory of ourselves as adults and as parents. We need to understand our character defects and the areas where we fall short as parents, and then work on those shortcomings with all our spirit. I get sick of people who always talk about family, yet are not willing to do the work to make theirs a real family.

I'm not preaching from on high. I had to learn these skills the hard way and there are still parenting issues I work on. But after raising eight kids, taking another five hundred into my home, and working with thousands of others at the Center over the years, I've gained some insight into what works and what doesn't. Here's a little of what I've learned.

Kids who have adults they can talk to honestly and openly aren't going to build bombs in the garage. You can learn a lot about your children — and from them — but first you have to be willing to listen. Really listen. And to listen well you've got to give up wanting to control everything about the child.

To get kids to talk with you openly, you have to keep your part of the bargain and be honest and open with them in return. Too often we try to cover up our defects and keep them hidden from our children. "I want you to respect me," we hammer into them over and over again, and we think that means we have to be something we are not. When you are willing to open up to children and share with them, you will be amazed at the things you learn about them. But you won't hear it if you're holding back and not telling them the whole truth. You've got to get real with kids.

That's true even with children as young as four or five years old. A father came into my house one day and dropped off his four-year-old son for me to watch while his mother was in the hospital having another baby. The dad set the kid's bag down and left, barely saying a word. This kid knew I was like a family member, and his dad wasn't out the door five minutes before the boy said, "Rose, why didn't my dad give you a hug? Why didn't he say anything?"

Sometimes this boy's dad was very cordial, helpful, and loving. At other times, he might fight you and curse you. Maybe he's bipolar.

There were a lot of things I wanted to tell this young boy, but instead I asked him, "Why don't you ask your dad?" So we waited until we thought the father was home and gave him a call. The young boy asked him, "Why did you come into Rose's house and not speak to her? And you didn't even hug Rose."

I couldn't hear what his father was saying on the other end of the line. All I knew was that this child wasn't buying it. He kept saying, "Mmm, mmm," but never "Okay." When I asked him what his dad said, he just shrugged his shoulders. Whatever the father said, it was so insignificant and off base that this four-year-old had dismissed it and couldn't even repeat it to me.

Most important, the father missed an opportunity to be honest with his child, to discuss something the child thought was important. Now, he may not have wanted to tell this young boy that he suffered from a mental illness, if he did, but he certainly could have told him he was in a bad mood or that he was angry or distracted about something. Kids understand that. Kids have their own moods; they have their own devils to deal with.

We all have defects, and hiding them from kids does children no good. Being honest about them is one way to open up a dialogue with kids, to find out what is bothering them, what their fears are, and what they want or need.

My kids knew I listened, but what they didn't know was how often I would go in my room and put my fist in my mouth to keep from screaming because of what they told me. I never let them see how disturbed I was because then they'd stop talking to me. As parents we sometimes have to know how to listen without reacting in stupid or predictable ways.

Parents don't have to be all-knowing and all-seeing. Loosen up, be human. My children, who are all over thirty now, tell me one of the things they liked most about me as a mother was that I didn't know it all. Do you know how good that makes me feel as a parent? They still talk about how I assisted them in discovering things and wouldn't get bent out of shape when they would come and talk to me about what was on their minds.

If they asked me something and I didn't know the answer, I would say, "Let's go to the library and find out," or "Let's ask Dr. Vinter (then a professor at the University of Michigan and the smartest man I knew at the time). Or I'd tell them we'd ask family friends.

You don't need to make all the decisions for your children or supply them with the "right answers." Give them space to make their own decisions, right and wrong. And give them time to express themselves.

A Zen Buddhist friend of mine tells me they have a saying that goes something like this: "The best way to control your sheep or cow is to give it a large spacious pasture." The same is true for children. Don't box them in. If you do you'll constantly be fighting over the boundaries of their little box. Give them space. Give them time. They'll learn how to wander around this "pasture" and you'll have a much easier time in helping them do so.

A woman brought her son to me recently because the courts had told him he was going to have to perform community service for something he'd done wrong. She and her husband are affluent people who are influential in the community. I knew her quite well from projects she had helped me on, but I didn't know her son, so I asked him a few questions: What do you want to be? What is it that got you in trouble? Was there a forewarning? Did you know you were getting ready to do it? Did you have an opportunity to change your decision?

Before he could answer any of the questions, momma piped up with the answer. Finally I couldn't take any more of it.

"Gerry, please," I said, "will you let Jay answer some of these questions. He's the one who's going to be doing the community service work, not you."

It was hard, but I could see by the way his eyes widened and a smile broke out on his face that we were now on the right track. I'm sure his mother didn't even realize what she was doing. But her son did.

A lot of good parents who otherwise raise their kids well want to make decisions for them. You can't do it. It won't work. That's why children do things their parents think is suddenly out of character. "That wasn't like her at all," they'd say about some misdeed. But the fact is they never trusted the child enough to really see his or her character for what it was. You don't know your child's character unless you let it bloom. You can water it. You can feed it. But you must let it bloom.

And when you ask a question, don't put the child on the spot to answer immediately. Be prepared to give them two or three minutes. Or say, "Think before you answer. Take your time. You don't have to answer right away, not even today if you don't want to." Give them room. Treat their answers with respect. Wait for signals. You can't spend fifteen or seventeen years encouraging your kids to know right from wrong and then not let them make a choice or express their opinions.

Give kids a sense of ownership in their home. I hear parents all the time who say something like, "You'll do this or that while you're in *my* house." Then they go on vacation and their seventeen-year-old has a beer or drug party, the house gets trashed, and maybe someone gets hurt or raped. Then they want to know how their Johnny could possibly have done such a thing. The answer is because they've made it *their* house, not *our* house.

Let the kids have a private world within the house. My kids knew that if they made it to the bedroom, mom wouldn't mess with them, even though there were times when I wanted to lob a Molotov cocktail in there.

One time I was chasing my son Joe through the house and would have strangled him, I swear, if I had caught him. But he made it to his room before I could—like sliding into home plate with the winning run in the World Series. Then he turned and looked over his shoulder to see if I would follow. I was madder than a hornet, but there was no way I was going to violate the safe haven of his room. Why? Because I didn't want him to feel he had to run away to some strange place to find sanctuary.

Another way to let kids know it's their home is to involve them in decisions about the house. If you're getting ready to buy furniture or paint, ask your kids what style or color they like. Show them samples. Take them shopping with you. Let them feel some ownership in the space and nine times out of ten they will protect it and not violate the rules.

Love should be sacred, unconditional. This is difficult for most adults to accept. But I believe it is the simple principle that would correct much of what's wrong with society today. The truth is, children give their parents this unconditional love more often than they receive it in return.

Too many parents want to put strings and conditions on their love. It's part of the control game. They think it gives them the ability to shape and form their children as they please. It doesn't. Believe me, I've talked with too many kids out of earshot of their parents to think otherwise.

Not long before my son got married, I had asked for a meeting between his future wife's family and ours. We met at a restaurant and both families were sitting there when the father of Joe's fiancée blasted his daughter in front of all of us.

"You think I sent you to college," he said to his daughter, "to end up marrying a damn bus driver? I wanted you to marry Jeffrey. That's what we were grooming you for. You were friends."

"But, Dad, Jeffrey beat me," she said.

"What did you do wrong?" he said.

"I didn't do nothing," she said. "People overlook his faults because he's popular, and the only reason he's so popular is because he has lots of money."

"You musta done something," he said. "You have totally disappointed your mother and me."

"Excuse me, I need to say something here," I said, and turned to my son. "Mr. Johnson is talking for himself and Mrs. Johnson. He is not talking for me. I love you very, very much, and I wouldn't care if you were on a viaduct with a shotgun shooting folks, you would still be my son. I love you, and I will be there for you. Don't ever worry about hearing anything like this from your mother. You don't always do things that I approve of or like, but you could never do anything to make me not love you."

Those skills did not come easily to me because I'd never known that kind of affection and support when I was young. It was awkward for me to hug my children when they were young—to give them physical reassurance. When I tried to hug them when they'd become adults, they would tighten up because they weren't accustomed to me touching them like that.

And I still find it difficult to accept when someone says they love me. Growing up, my inner voice was always saying, "Take care of yourself or they'll kill you or get rid of you. Nobody likes you." I saw too many people professing love and doing the most despicable things. Tell me you admire me or that you think I'm a great person. I can accept that. Tell me you respect me or like me. But if you tell me you love me and I know you don't, I will quarrel with you because I can't handle people telling others they love them when they haven't a clue what that means.

For me, telling someone I love them means taking on a hell of a responsibility. I have to show that love all the time. There's no walking away. There's no "I love you but you've got to do things my way."

Love is sacred. And that's how it should be with our children.

A Love Story

So let me tell you a real love story that says something not only about people in love but the unconditional love of parents.

Ben and Angela were students at Huron High School who fell in love with each other in the eleventh grade. Ben was a white kid whose parents were very wealthy. Angela was a black girl whose mother got married when she was about fourteen, had seven children, and got divorced. Now that Angela was a teenager, the mother—now about thirty years old—had regressed and was acting like the teenager she never got a chance to be. She was always going to a party, and if she had ten dollars, she'd buy herself a blouse or a pair of shoes, not something for her kids.

It was obvious that Ben's father didn't want him to have a relationship with Angela. I don't think he was prejudiced. I believe he just felt that Angela's life was too troubled. During the second year of their courtship, Angela got pregnant. Ben's parents— who'd already taken a beating from neighbors, friends, and business associates about Ben's courtship with this black girl from public housing—were thrown for a loop. But they stood up under the pressure because Ben's happiness was more important to them than anything.

First Ben's parents asked him what he would like to do about the pregnancy. When Ben told them they were going to keep the baby and get married, as deeply as it must have pained them, they sat back, smiled, and congratulated him for taking the mature approach to the situation. They were especially relieved that he didn't plan on dropping out of school.

Then Ben's parents did what good soon-to-be grandparents should do: they got Angela into the prenatal clinic and started buying clothes and baby accessories for the couple.

When Angela went into labor, she called me. Ben was going to be her coach, and I was going to be there to help. Ben, Angela's mom, Ben's parents, and I were all in the delivery room. Ben and I were coaching Angela and the grandparents-to-be were waiting anxiously on the side. It was a long, hard labor, but when the nurse finally put the baby in young Ben's arms he kissed the baby and started dancing around the room in pure joy. When the grandparents got their chance to hold the baby they were just as giddy with excitement. Oh, it was something.

But that baby, it was obvious to me—and anyone who had an ounce of sense—was 100 percent black. Not an ounce of Caucasian blood in him. Afterward, I could tell Ben's mom and dad knew it too.

"Liz Taylor and Richard Burton shouldn't get the Academy Awards this year," I told them later. "You two should."

They told me they were not about to let Ben see any doubt or disappointment in their eyes. They wanted him to come to grips with this situation himself. His happiness was more important than the excruciating pain they felt, especially after all they'd done for Angela and her family during the pregnancy.

That was a hell of a show of character. What parents.

Ben showed the baby around proudly for a couple of weeks, but after he'd heard enough friends—black and white—tell him "Ben, this baby doesn't look anything like you," he went to his dad and asked if he'd pay to get a blood test. His father assured him he would do whatever Ben wanted.

Angela swore by God and two white men—which is valid in any court—that this was Ben's baby. She wasn't the type of kid to lie, but she desperately wanted Ben to be the father. She knew that he'd be the best father for her baby and that he had a solid future ahead of him. She had had sex with Ben and someone else, but I think she really convinced herself that Ben was the dad.

The blood test came back and showed there was one chance in two billion it was Ben's baby. Angela cried and cried and cried. Later a couple of her friends came to me and told me it was Bo Taylor's baby, and the first words out of my mouth were, "Oh, shit." Bo always had a sweet look on his face, dressed well, and was well groomed. He wasn't the type of guy who'd cause you to hold your purse tighter when you saw him, but this kid had a knack for getting in trouble and staying in trouble. Since then, he's been in and out of the penitentiary and ended up having seven or eight kids around town who are being raised without a father.

Ben's parents told Angela she could keep all the baby paraphernalia they had bought, and they helped her through the first stages of motherhood with baby formula and Pampers. They even gave the baby a college tuition voucher. They didn't just quit when they learned it wasn't their son's baby. They—and Ben—

weaned themselves from the situation in a loving, honorable, supportive way.

Ben's dad told me: "When a lot of my close friends balked at the fact that I was setting up this fund for the baby to go to college, I said, 'You don't understand. My son loved this young girl.' It is more important for me to stay on the same page with my son." Ben was ecstatic his father had made that gesture for the child.

Ben's parents showed the kind of true unconditional love that bonds a child to his parents. They let him make his own choices and they stood behind him.

THE BATHROOM AT THE REEDS' HOME—*where my brothers and sisters and I had been sent to live after my mother died—was on the first floor and had a little window in it that opened to the outside.*

When I would take baths in there, Mr. Reed would often come by, open the window, and look in at me. I was always the feisty one in the family, and I'd shout at him to get away from the window. Sometimes I'd throw water in his face and say, "I'm going to tell," to get him to run away. Those seemed to be the magic words to stop him, because Mr. Reed liked to be thought of as an upstanding man in the community.

Other times, he'd be in there and call me to the window. When I came over, there he'd be standing completely naked.

He never violated me, and I was in my fifties before I learned that he had raped one of my sisters. Words cannot describe the pain I felt on learning that. My sister. The one I had sworn to my mother I would take care of.

"Doll Baby—that was her nickname—why didn't you tell me. I would have killed him."

She looked up at me and said, "That's why I didn't. I knew you would."

And she was right, I would have.

SEVEN

Creative Fundraising

$\mathcal{I}$'M KNOWN FOR MY unconventional methods, but there have been times when they were more unconventional than most people would imagine.

Please understand, I deal with two worlds: the haves, whom I ask to provide resources, and the have-nots, who are in need of services. It's not unusual for the haves to want some control over how their money is spent—either who gets it, how much they get, or what it's used for. Sometimes they attach conditions to their generosity. And often lurking just below the surface is the issue of sex. Any woman who has approached the wealthy and powerful for help knows that sex is going to come up before long.

I've had them make all kinds of crazy offers. I had one guy who I hoped would get a program started for me because all his peers were millionaires. I'd been trying to establish a project where millionaires would meet at Peace Neighborhood Center once a month for a lunch that I would prepare, and then my clients, staff, and I would update them on our goals for the next month. It would give them a chance to interact directly with some of our clients.

I was sitting in the old Wonder Bar with this guy—I was having a kiddie cocktail while he drank a few beers—telling him about my program and trying to hold onto him because I had no rapport with anyone else who could set this up. I was telling him about all the services we provide for the city, and suddenly he blurted out that he would see to it that my program got $50,000 if I would have sex with his girlfriend. That was in 1979, so you can imagine how much money that would be today. Needless to say, I told him to get lost and that was our last conversation.

About the same time, another man got in touch with me about making a major contribution to the Center. Somehow the money never materialized, but he would keep dangling it in front of me like a carrot. I was excited that someone of his means was thinking of becoming a patron of what I was doing, so naturally I didn't want to piss him off. I spent a good deal of time with him, and twice he took me to dinner.

Then it came out: his wife had seen me make a presentation, got the hots for me, and had sent him after me. He would give me the money only if he could see me in bed with his wife. I turned him down flat. But he kept fattening the pot, adding more money. I remember him saying to me, "There's a price for everything. Now this might not be your forte, and it might not be what you would normally do, but a price will get you everything. And I know you're a hustler."

By then, the pot was up to something like $35,000.

I thought about it carefully and went over it with my girlfriend. Then I told him, "You got me dead right: I am a hustler, but I'm not a whore. And you got this wrong: money will not buy this fantasy."

A week or two later, I called him and told him he owed me money anyway for the time I'd been spending with him while he had a covert agenda. I think I reached his conscience, because he ended up giving us $8,000.

Another wealthy businessman, educated at one of the best Ivy League schools, used to be one of my guardian angels, a person I could go to in a real emergency and count on his coming through. I was crazy about him because I liked his heart, but he did have one outrageous behavior. Whenever I would go into his private office—a very nice, plush office with a big old desk—he would always be wearing a sport jacket, tie, long-sleeved shirt, socks, shoes, and his watch. No underwear. No trousers. He would walk around his office that way like he was fully clothed.

This was during the days of the sexual revolution when people were streaking in public and otherwise breaking out of their strait-laced lives in strange ways. Other than that idiosyncrasy, he never did anything wrong, never made a move on me. I don't know if he was dressed (or undressed) this way all the time, but he was always that way when I was in his office. He was nice and he shared what he had with other people, so I never asked him to explain.

One day I was headed to Mammoth Cave in Kentucky with a busload of forty-seven kids. We were packed and ready to go when I learned of a fifty-nine-year-old woman who needed help quickly because she was about to lose her home. She had become sick and couldn't work, but she wasn't old enough to get her retirement or sick enough to receive her Social Security. She had quickly used up what little she had saved. The bottom line was she needed $4,000, now.

Not wanting this lady to lose her home while we were out of town, I whipped the bus over to the office of my friend and benefactor, the pantless executive. I told the kids to stay in the bus.

I went in, and his secretary, whom I adored, said right away, "Rose, you may go in." As I sat in his office trying to explain why I needed the money, kids started getting off the bus and coming into the waiting room—wanting water, wanting to use the bathroom, wanting to know where I was.

Suddenly, there were a dozen kids out there. All the while he—dressed in his usual style—was reaching all over his desk looking for his checkbook, pushing papers on the floor. Now, black people have myths about white people, and white people have myths about black people. One myth I had heard about white men was that they aren't hung. Well, that was not the case with this white man.

Finally he came out from behind the desk, shuffling through the stuff he'd thrown on the floor. As

ONE ROSE BLOOMING

usual, he was acting like there was nothing strange about this at all. But I kept putting my head out the door to tell the children to calm down and get back in the bus. Every time I looked out the door, there were more kids. The waiting room was filling up fast.

Finally he pulled the checkbook out from one of the piles of paper on the floor and wrote me a check for the $4,000. I dashed for the kids and the bus before they started spilling into his office. Only then did I breathe a sigh of relief.

Some of my friends have wondered why I dealt with somebody like that. I told them it was his business if he wanted to walk around half naked, as long as he wrote the check and people got served.

And it isn't just men. I knew a woman whose husband was a research doctor who traveled all the time. One day we were at the Interfaith Council Congregation giving some big whatever, and I was there making a pitch for Peace Neighborhood Center.

She was filthy rich and had five grown children.

"There's something I want to talk to you about," she said. So I set up an appointment for her to come to my office. I was hoping she wanted to talk about getting involved in some of our programs.

When she came to my office, it was clear she had something else on her mind. At first she seemed to be coming on to me, dragging her words out and all. Then she told me she loved her husband and her family very much—and I breathed a sigh of relief—but she had noticed the increase in interracial relationships in Ann Arbor. She'd gone over her life and the only thing she hadn't experienced was a relationship with a black man.

"Is that all you want," I said. Then I added right away, "Well, I'm trying to raise money to take these kids to Washington to visit Congress and the Lincoln Memorial. I'm five thousand dollars short. I could help you — probably give you some tips — but that's not a priority right now. My kids are, though."

"Look," she said, "the kids will go to Washington. Talk to me about this. I'm coming to you because you're a trusted member of the community."

"Does this mean you are going to give me the five thousand?" I asked.

"Five thousand, five thousand. Is that what you need?" she asked. "Let's get this out of the way so we can talk." And she wrote the check right then — the fastest five thousand bucks I had ever raised, and to see her write the check from her personal checking account was almost too much to bear. I started getting nauseous, but I fought it back and tried to maintain my cool.

Of course, I still had to earn my "consulting fee," or whatever it was.

"I will talk to anyone you want me to talk to," I said. "Do you have anybody in mind?"

"Well," she said, "in my volunteer responsibilities throughout the city, I've seen a couple, but I could never approach anybody and suggest anything like this." She told me she didn't want to fall in love and run off and get married. She just wanted to experience it.

"It's going to take great discipline on your part," I said. "You could be in a world of trouble before you know it." I also gave her a talk about all the spiritual ramifications of infidelity and adultery, and I was sincere about it.

"I didn't come here to go to church," she shot back at me. "If I wanted religious consultation, I'd have gone to talk to my pastor. I want somebody to talk this through with me...and to keep it under wraps."

So I helped her, and I won't say how even now. Why would I do such a thing? Because I figured it was up to her to look after her own character. My eyes were fixed on the light that I would see in the eyes of the forty-seven housing project kids when they got a chance to see their nation's Capitol.

Another person I came to know was head of a corporation that hired people in our employment programs at Peace Neighborhood Center. The people he hired had little or no marketable skills and would make $10 to $14 an hour with a high school education. As a result of this employment, good things happened to them. They bought homes, elevated themselves in the community.

I tried to involve this executive more in our programs, to introduce him to people. Although he kept coming to meetings I was attending and served on committees with me, I felt that somehow I wasn't getting through to him. I wasn't communicating. He just seemed to be going through the motions, biding his time.

Then one night he had me meet him at his office. He told me he wanted to make a financial contribution to the program. He'd write a check on the spot for $10,000. I about fell over. Man, I thought, this is too good to be true. In a way it was.

He scribbled out a check and started to hand it to me. Then he pulled it back, teasingly. Well, maybe there was just one more thing, he said. I asked him what and he hemmed and hawed, then started to hand the check over again. And again pulled it back. What is going on, I wondered. Then he blurted it out. "I'll give you the ten thousand dollars if you let me see your breasts," he said. He told me they captivated him. I was about thirty-three at the time and I was gorgeous — I ain't lying.

Suddenly it dawned on me why he kept coming to those meetings and serving on those committees. He had a hidden agenda. He didn't want our contact to be over because he wanted to see my boobs. I was too bright for him to openly proposition me, and he was too much of a coward.

"You're not talking about physically touching me, are you?" I asked.

"No, I just want to see them," he said, sliding the $10,000 check across his desk pad. "You can call the bank and find out if it's any good."

"That won't be necessary," I told him. "If I show you my tits, I'm going to get my money. If not, you'll get your ass kicked. You'll see a different side of Rose Martin."

So I showed him, and he was like a kid at the circus. He wasn't masturbating or anything like that, but it was like he had just hit the lottery. I guess he had too much money and not enough good things to do with it.

When I told my sister what I did, she said, "No, you did not. Rose Martin, you can't do things like that."

"Guess what?" I said. "I'm done for the week. I don't have to crawl under any more rocks trying to get money for this program."

As I was walking out, I told her, "Honey, I've only got one problem with what happened."

"What's that?"

"There might be twenty men in this town who would give ten thousand dollars to see my boobs," I said, "and I've only identified one of them."

EIGHT

Moving On Up

I WAS DELIGHTED when Mr. Canfield called and told me he wanted Peace Neighborhood Center to help him with his upcoming move. One of the services the Center provides is temporary employment for recovering addicts. In addition to moving people's belongings, we cater weddings, do drop-in baby-sitting, and perform similar jobs. Many of the recovering addicts have expertise in various skilled trades—as electricians, plumbers, and contractors, and we've even built a couple of homes for about half the price that others would charge.

Although we certainly are no employment agency—and don't want to be—these jobs give recovering addicts enough pocket change while they are in recovery to cover their personal expenses—bus tokens, telephone cards, gas, shaving cream, cigarettes, and the like. Only clients who have been screened and have been in recovery for a while are eligible for the work programs.

Mr. Canfield explained that he needed our services the next day; the sale of his house was contingent on his being out by then. He was a professor who had been generous to the Center. Although he'd never given us money directly, he had been a splendid advocate of the Center, promoting our cause to various community groups.

Our golden rule in taking moving jobs is that we always make a site visit and assess the job before quoting a price. But Mr. Canfield was in a hurry and I'd known him for years and trusted him. He said he had a standard three-bedroom home—nothing special involved. So I agreed to charge him $600, assuming it would take three or four guys five or six hours.

The next morning the crew assembled and we arrived at Mr. Canfield's house at 8:45 A.M. We took a quick look around and knew immediately we were in trouble. I'll concede that technically the house did have three bedrooms. Mr. Canfield was right about that. But there were also two living rooms, a recreation room, and a laundry room, not to mention a piano, freezers, washing machines, and a solid hardwood, floor-to-ceiling bar front—the kind you'd find in a hotel—that weighed thousands of pounds.

And the house was brimming with a lifetime collection of beautiful antique furniture. Heavy, awkward antique furniture. It was all solid oak or solid maple. I don't think he owned a thing that weighed less than fifty pounds.

The crew was ready to mutiny.

"Six hundred dollars for that?" one of them said. "That man's crazy. We're going to have to bring in at least two more guys, and we'll still be on this for two days. Nobody in the world would move him for less than three or four thousand dollars."

"I've used Peace Neighborhood Center's name," I said, "and he has to be out today. Forgive me, please."

They knew they were being ripped off, and so did I. But after a few minutes of grumbling among themselves, Dexter spoke for the group.

"We'll move him because you used Peace's name," he said, and the others nodded approval. For guys who had spent much of their lives avoiding things like loyalty and responsibility, it was a big step. I was overwhelmed and nearly in tears.

"Maybe he'll realize how much he's underestimated the job once we get started," I said, trying to put a positive spin on it. "Maybe he'll give us another five hundred or a thousand once he sees how dedicated we are in getting the job done."

The crew jumped into the task with all the enthusiasm they could muster. I had not called on our top movers—some of whom had experience with professional moving companies—because I thought the job would be routine. But the crew I had was a hardworking group that included my son Joe, one of the best movers I know.

Mr. Canfield, I'll concede, did his fair share of lifting and hauling. He worked beside us all day. At two o'clock we broke for lunch and I ordered sandwiches from Zingerman's Delicatessen for all of us, including Mr. Canfield. That cost $60, so our already paltry $600 was down to $540.

Three o'clock—the time we thought we'd be done—passed with only a dent having been made in the job. By five o'clock we were about halfway done, and at midnight the job that should have taken two or more days was complete. We limped home. Two of the movers were guys who were staying at my home while they waited for beds to open up in a treatment center.

I fell into bed dead-tired. Although the men had been doing all the heavy work, I'd been there to support them, get lunch, baby-sit for one guy's four-year-old son, and generally do what I could to bail us out of the situation. I wasn't in bed long when I heard a loud commotion in the kitchen downstairs. I went down, ready to read them the riot act for not letting me sleep, to discover that Dexter, one of the movers who wasn't staying with me, had come over.

"Rose," I heard Dexter say through my half-sleep, "when we were moving Mr. Canfield today, James broke one of the chairs. It was one of eight antique chairs from the dining room set."

Dexter told me James had thrown the broken chair into a construction Dumpster at Mr. Canfield's new house. The house was still under construction and we moved the furniture into the lower level until the house was completed. But Dexter couldn't sleep because he was worried that throwing the antique chair away was the wrong thing to do.

I told him we at least needed to tell Mr. Canfield. But Michael, one of the men staying at my house, suggested we get in the van, go over to the new house, and see if we could get the chair out. Then we'd try to find someone to fix it.

I had my doubts about the plan. For one thing, I was scared to death some ignorant cop would show up, miss the point of what we were doing, and wreak havoc. But it was late, I was so tired I couldn't think straight, and I couldn't see any other way around the problem. So off we went—me in my nightgown and robe accompanied by these ex-cons and recovering addicts to this posh neighborhood where poor people aren't expected to be hanging around in the daylight, much less the middle of the night.

We hoisted Dexter up over the edge of the Dumpster to do his Dumpster-diving and heard him hit bottom with a reassuring *thunk*. It was pitch black but the moon slipped out from behind the clouds just as Dexter started scavenging through the junk, giving him enough light to find the various parts of the broken chair. We stacked up parts as fast as he threw them out, all of us frightened that at any moment we'd be busted.

Finally we had all the pieces, and the only challenge remaining was to get Dexter out of the Dumpster. By forming a human chain we were able to reach down and haul him over the edge, and we all beat a hasty retreat.

Two days later we found someone in a Detroit suburb to look at the chair. It could be fixed, he said, for $300, but according to him the chair was valued at $700 and worth the effort. Our $540 profit had just shrunk to $240, minus the gas to take the chair to the repair shop.

Four days later we got the repaired chair back and I gave Mr. Canfield a call. I asked him to come to my office and when he got there I told him the story of the chair. I could see he was visibly upset when I described the chair being thrown in the Dumpster. Then I gave my assistant a signal and he brought the repaired chair out of the closet.

Mr. Canfield looked it over carefully and started to laugh, almost maniacally, with relief. He couldn't see any sign of the repairs, he said.

He stood up with tears in his eyes, clutched the chair to his chest, and said, "Rose Martin, you are such a wonderful person. You are Ann Arbor's Mother Teresa. Thank you, thank you, thank you." He hugged his chair again, put it in his van, and took off.

I wanted him to appreciate the love, concern, and sensitivity the men who moved him had shown. I hoped he would recognize that this was something they surely wouldn't have felt prior to entering recovery. I wanted him to know that they had all voted to take the repair money out of what he had paid us, even though they had worked many more hours than they had been paid for.

I wanted him to understand that if you take the time to treat people well, they will behave well. But all he left with was a repaired chair and a missed opportunity at growth.

A few weeks later one of the men in the moving crew stopped in to see me.

"You know, Rose, that move was painful, watching that man take advantage of us like that. We could say fuck Mr. Canfield because he fucked us, but we aren't going to do it that way. We may be powerless over the Mr. Canfields of the world, but somehow it feels good to do what's right."

Mr. Canfield had moved into his new million-dollar home and was by now probably polishing his antiques and feeling smug about the deal he'd cut with us. But my ragtag group of recovering addicts had made a more important move—one toward pride, self-respect, and integrity.

I REALLY LOOKED UP TO MY AUNT LU. She had a beautiful house, always had a new car, and dressed nice.

Every Friday night Aunt Lu and my other aunts and uncles would gather at the kitchen table and start drinking. They'd drink from the time they got off work on Friday until Sunday, when they'd quit and get ready to go back to work. Come Friday they'd start all over again. For them it was a big thing to be able to drink and hold your liquor without clowning or fighting or trifling. Straight liquor, that's all they'd drink. No "sissy drinks" like the white people would have.

With my momma and daddy gone, and me living in a string of foster homes where nobody gave a damn about me, I dreamed of sitting at that table with Aunt Lu and her friends. And oh how I wanted that woman to praise me and think highly of me. Even though I was getting very good grades in school, no one ever had a kind word to say to me.

Well, one day Aunt Lu got word that I'd been going out with some older friends and had been drinking a lot. Most important to her, she heard I'd held my liquor well. I was about twenty at the time, and I was practicing with my friends to be like my Aunt Lu. She was my role model and I wanted to drink like her—straight liquor with no mix or water. I wanted to sit at that table with my aunts and uncles and have their approval.

One day they were in there and she said to me, "I heard you drinkin' red liquor. Let me see if you can drink." Red liquor was what they called dark whiskey like Four Roses. And I sat down at that table and I drank with her. Now, my Aunt Lu could drink her way through a whole lot of whiskey in an evening. But every time she would take a drink, I had to take a drink. Before that evening was over, I was so sick I just wanted to jump out that window. But I was going to show her I could hold my liquor. After we'd finished a few bottles, she was beaming with pride. "They're right, you can drink girl! I told your momma before she died that you was like me."

Aunt Lu's praise washed over me like a warm breeze. Here I was, twenty years old, and Aunt Lu was the first person I ever felt accepted me.

And I was sick, but I would not allow myself to throw up or go crazy in her presence. I was so glad when the liquor was gone, I just prayed and called on everything that was holy in the universe to help me out of her front room.

I went to the door and she was sitting there drunk on the couch with her hands curled up—when she was drunk the only thing you'd notice would be that her hands curled up like she was having a seizure—and she said, "You're **my** niece. All right, we are of the same cloth."

I stepped out that door and threw up and fell down along her white fence. And a cab driver came along and said, "Ma'am, do you want me to get you to the hospital." I said, "**Hurry up** and get me somewhere, **I'm dying**."

The shit had only just begun. She wanted to show me to the world as the kid who could drink that much alcohol and not clown, not throw up, and not have my personality change that much. She'd brag on me constantly and put me up against men who thought they were the drinkers of the century. She'd say, "My niece can outdrink your ass." She'd set it up and get a ten-dollar bet, which was a lot of money in those days. And I felt I had to win because I didn't want her to lose that money. And I wanted her approval. No matter what would happen, I would outdrink them. On occasion, Aunt Lu would share some of her winnings with me.

So I would take Monday through Thursday to recuperate—puking, runny bowels, the whole thing—and then it would be Friday and time to do it again.

She'd take me around the neighborhoods, to the park, or to the house parties in people's homes, and she would make her bets on me. Sometimes the party would last all night before a winner was declared. She'd even drive me in that car of hers to other cities along the coast. And a lot of times people would come to her home saying, "Where the hell is this person I'm supposed to outdrink?"

"You cannot outdo my baby," she'd say. And I wanted to hear that. I needed to hear her approval, even though I'd be sick as a dog. I didn't have nobody that gave a damn about me.

NINE

Cooking Up Commerce

*I*T WAS A BRILLIANT IDEA. A natural. A sure thing. I planned to open a restaurant in downtown Ann Arbor with the help of kids from the Peace Neighborhood Center and a few friends. Not only would the restaurant give kids a place to learn good work habits, it would keep them off the street corners, instill a sense of pride that comes from working on your own project, and give them some much-needed money. Since restaurant work was one of the few jobs available to these clients, many already had experience.

I would be the cook; the kids would do everything else. I knew I was qualified to do the cooking because I'd been doing it all my adult life and people seemed to love it. As early as 1978 I had been working evenings to earn money to start the restaurant. At first, I worked with the kids at the Center doing catering jobs. Then I started cooking Wednesday nights at a popular restaurant on the outskirts of town. I'd take a couple of kids with me and we'd run the whole kitchen that night. The restaurant would advertise that Rose Martin would be cooking, and piles of people would come in.

By 1985 I had an even larger group of kids thirteen to fifteen years old who started pushing me about working in the restaurant. They all had some past experience at McDonald's or Colonel Sanders or Wendy's. So I doubled the nights I cooked at the restaurant and increased the money I was putting away for the dream of a place of our own.

Then the brilliant idea I'd been carrying around for more than eight years began to jell. I heard that Nick, who owned a restaurant called the Cloverleaf, was selling his business. It was on Huron Street, one of the city's main arteries, and directly across from the newspaper, the *Ann Arbor News*. I went to talk with Nick and before long we cut a deal for me to buy the restaurant—equipment, supplies, licenses, and all. Although the money I'd saved working at night over the last eight years wasn't enough to pay for it outright, several supporters kicked in money and Nick and I worked out terms that would let me pay for the equipment and supplies over time. I would assume Nick's lease on the place.

I mapped out a business plan. I talked to other restaurant owners. Things began to fall in place. It looked like we were about to hit pay dirt.

The carpenters union was on strike at the time we

were revamping the restaurant, so a couple of friends who belonged to that union came down and worked day and night for free—I only had to pay for materials. We did the restaurant in Southern country-kitchen style. My girlfriend Nondi and I put together a soul food and Cajun menu that included cornbread, jambalaya, shrimp Creole, sweet potato pie, ham hocks, red beans and rice, barbecue chicken and ribs, and a variety of other home-cooking-style meals. We visited other restaurants to come up with comparable prices for our meals. The idea for the restaurant also struck a favorable chord with the local media, and we began to receive some very nice advance publicity.

Finally we had the place the way we wanted it. We called it the Rosebowl. It was shining, nearly ready for business. About 8:30 in the morning the day before we were to open, the Miesel-Sysco truck pulled up in front of the restaurant to deliver our supplies so we could start preparing food for the opening. A nice man named John got out and handed me an invoice for $3,400. I didn't have the money on hand since we'd run over on the cost of materials we had put into refurbishing the place. So I just signed the invoice and started walking back to the kitchen.

"You have to pay me before I unload the truck," John announced. "You're a new account and they don't let new accounts get credit right off."

We were one day from opening and we couldn't pay for the food or get it on credit. I should have seen the handwriting on the wall and handed the keys to the landlord right then and there. Instead, I looked at

John and told him we didn't have the money on hand.

He looked in the restaurant and saw all those kids from the projects working hard on last-minute details. "I'll tell you what," he said. "I'll make all my other deliveries and be back around five-thirty or six this evening. That will give you the rest of the day to get the money."

I started frantically calling friends to explain the bind I was in. Unfortunately, many of them were out of town because it was shortly after Labor Day. I did manage to get hold of one person I knew—a philanthropist who gave money to youth activities designed to prepare kids for business. He told me to come to his house in Barton Hills and talk about it. So I drove out to one of Ann Arbor's most exclusive neighborhoods to see Millard and Mary Pryor. After standing in their living room pleading my case, Mrs. Pryor looked at her husband and said, "Millard, let's loan them the money."

Mr. Pryor had been looking over the business plan I brought and said it seemed like a good one. But was I aware, he asked, how hard the kids and I were going to have to work? I assured him that we'd worked hard for years to raise money and we'd do so in the future. That was good enough for him, and he wrote us a check for the loan on the spot.

When John came back with the food truck, I handed him a cashier's check to cover the invoice and we unloaded our first supplies amidst a whole lot of screaming and laughing and carrying on. The kids and I immediately started cooking because we had to have the menu ready for the grand opening the following day. We called on some friends of Peace Neighborhood Center to come down and help out. We not only cooked up some fine food, but a great feeling of unity and friendship simmered and bubbled inside the restaurant that night and it gave off an intoxicating aroma that was just as sweet as the smell of barbecued ribs, our homemade fruit butter, and country-fried chicken.

While we were in the midst of food preparation, a blue-eyed, blond-haired boy who didn't look a day over twelve years old walked into this soul-food scene and announced that he was looking for a job.

Say what? I thought.

"You're not old enough to look for a job, let alone hold one," I told him.

"I know, but my dad says I need to start. I need to work a little bit."

"Can you count?" I asked.

He nodded that he could.

"Okay," I said. "You're our cashier."

His name was Jon and he came two days a week to run the cash register. We set a milk crate behind the counter for him to stand on so he could reach the keys on the register. He was a wonderful kid, and he fit in perfectly and got along well with everyone. Jon and one other person were the only people who ever got paid. The kids from the neighborhood, my own children, various friends, and I never received a dime.

We opened in good spirits and got a wonderful review about the restaurant in the *Ann Arbor News*. We were riding high on the glamour of this new venture. But Mr. Pryor was right—this was hard work. My friends came to understand that if they wanted to see me, they had to come to the restaurant. I'd be making pies or frying chicken, and if they stayed any length of time, they'd be peeling potatoes right along beside me. There was no room for idle hands.

Then the reality of running a restaurant smacked me in the face like a plate of hot mashed potatoes. There was a big difference, I was learning, between cooking in someone else's restaurant one or two nights a week and having all the responsibility of running one of your own. Despite our good food, we didn't have enough money. Liability insurance was horrendous. Meeting health regulations was expensive, too. The rent was a thousand dollars a month, but suddenly a new month seemed to come around much faster than I'd ever seen one arrive before. Our landlord was unbending. He didn't care anything about our business beyond collecting the money.

Our biggest problem was parking. We had solicited advice in preparing our business plan from Cliff Sheldon, an executive with First of America Bank at the time. I can remember him telling me the three keys to a successful restaurant: location, location, location. And every day I was in that restaurant, I realized how right he was. Not only weren't there any legal parking spaces nearby for sit-down traffic, but the police department was next door and their parking lot was adjacent to the back of our restaurant. They were always there, and when we tried to build up our take-out business, they were towing and ticketing cars that were parked for only a few minutes. We thought about making deliveries, but without enough money to pay the bills, launching a new service was out of the question.

Then one day as we were in the kitchen cooking, we heard a humming noise and everything went pitch black. Detroit Edison had turned off our electricity. At lunchtime. One of the kids came running from the backyard and said he had just seen a man in a Detroit Edison uniform climbing down the pole, so I sent him down the street to find this man and have him come back to the restaurant.

"What's the deal?" I asked.

"The deal is you owe five hundred dollars and you haven't paid it," he said.

"Can't you leave it on until the end of the day?"

"No," he said, "but if you can get the money to Detroit Edison today, I'll come back by the end of the day and turn it back on. Otherwise, you're going to have to go through the system and that could take several days."

I couldn't help but think back to the day before we opened and the favor that John, the food deliveryman, had done us. This time things seemed more desperate. The Peace Neighborhood Center had recently laid in a couple of cases of candles to give to people if the city got hit by a big storm and the power went out. We got the candles, lit them, and put them on customers' tables to get through the lunch rush. Everyone took this little unexpected romantic touch in good spirits.

After the lunch crowd thinned, I started running around town trying to find a way to pay the light bill. Just when I thought I had exhausted every possible resource, I ran into a friend who said he'd go to his boss, get his paycheck early, and pay the Detroit Edison bill in person.

By the next day we were back in business, cooking up a storm for the lunch crowd. Within a week, just as we were hitting our stride, the fires on the stove died. The gas was out. At first we thought something terrible had happened, that the place might explode at any minute. We scrambled under stoves and behind refrigerators looking for a broken gas line. Then in the back door came a man from MichCon to tell us the gas lines had been shut off until the bill was paid.

We had fifteen orders to cook, and I didn't need any gas to get *me* hot. I started arguing and carrying on with him out of complete frustration, but then I realized he was just doing his job and I certainly didn't want the homeless people jumping in to settle things.

Luckily, we had two microwaves, and the orders were primarily for food coming out of the refrigerator that I had cooked the night before. We heated and served it. Then I got on the phone crying to my brother, my sister, anyone who knew me. When I got home that night, tired and discouraged, I found five one-hundred-dollar bills in my mailbox. There was no note or letter of explanation. When I asked around, one of the neighbors said she'd seen my best friend, Mary, stop at the mailbox earlier. Mary worked all day as a nurse and on her days off volunteered to help in the restaurant supervising kids. The next day at the restaurant I asked her if she'd left the money, but she brushed off the topic — said she didn't want to talk about it — and jumped back into work.

By now the roof was leaking, something the seller hadn't bothered to tell me about when I bought the restaurant. But it was my responsibility now under terms of the lease. We used some of our pots from the kitchen to catch the leaks, but we knew we wouldn't stay open long that way once the health department came by for its regular checkups.

Then another miracle came our way. My friend Papa Shed called and said he had an aunt who had just died and left him $2,000. Papa Shed had not seen that kind of money in his entire life. He was one of the poorest people I knew, although whenever you saw him on the street he always had his bib overalls full of pencils and paperback books to give to children.

"Rose Martin," he said, "they just delivered the check today. It's still warm from the mailman's bag, and I'm on my way down to give it to you." That was Papa Shed for you, a sure-enough friend of anyone in need despite his own impoverished condition.

We got things going again and we did manage to have some fun. Sometimes customers would come in and ask for something we didn't have — the name of something they'd heard was soul food but they didn't have a clue what it should look like or how it should taste. The people working in the restaurant, knowing we needed all the business we could get, would come back to me and say, "Rose, what are we going to do? We don't have that."

"We do now," I'd say. "Watch this." And I'd put together something and the customer would invariably say, "Oooohh, this is great," and go away well satisfied.

The restaurant venture had been a rocky road, but we came up with an idea that would put us on the highway to success. All-you-can-eat menus were just becoming popular in the mid-1980s. We decided that every Saturday we'd offer the world's best, down-home all-you-can-eat soul food for five bucks a plate. What's more, we'd advertise it to the athletes at the University of Michigan and they, in turn, would attract others. We just knew that a lot of those football and basketball players and other athletes who had been raised in the inner city would be ravenous for some home-cooked cornbread, barbecued ribs and chicken, collard greens, and black-eyed peas.

We had the kids hand out menus on campus to students and athletes announcing the Saturday $5.00 all-you-can-eat special, along with coupons that let you bring a friend for $2.50. Then we fired up the stove twenty-four hours before our scheduled opening at noon Saturday and started preparation. When the day arrived, we looked out the door just before we were to open and a large line had already formed. Cheers went up from the staff. The Rosebowl would be saved.

Do you have any idea how much food a 275-pound lineman can eat in one sitting? Lord have mercy, I didn't. And I'm not sure there *is* a limit to it. Those hungry athletes and students just inhaled that food. A full day's preparation disappeared before our eyes. We kept bringing it out and they kept shoveling it down. And what they didn't eat went to waste. Unlike prefabricated or semi-prepared food which is mostly air and salt, this was home-cooked stick-to-your-ribs food. But they'd pile it on their plates like they were eating hot dogs or cotton candy. We ended up scraping more than five dollars' worth of food into the garbage, and who knows the value of what disappeared into those cavernous bellies.

But we were not about to admit defeat. Like those athletes, we needed a victory in the Rosebowl. So we prepared even harder for the next Saturday, although this time we didn't advertise it to the athletes. And when we opened the doors, do you know who showed up? An entire basketball team from another city, along with the band and the cheerleaders and the team's fans.

People were spilling out of the Rosebowl onto the street. All told there were maybe a couple hundred people, and we quickly burned through the food we'd prepared. In desperation I heated up a large pot of oil and started frying chicken, and we kept running fried chicken and more fried chicken out to that hungry team and its supporters. Of course, the more we cooked and served, the faster we were headed toward bankruptcy.

I knew it was time to get out from under this restaurant. Nick told me to put an ad in the paper and somebody would buy it in a few days because it was a prime location.

"If you find the buyer yourself, you can at least get some of your money back," he said.

Some lawyers, however, advised me to give Nick the keys, walk away, and file for bankruptcy. I took that advice. Two days after I gave him the keys to the Rosebowl, he had another owner moving in. It turned out Nick's advice was right—and it may have been the *only* honest thing he told me about the restaurant.

Nine months after it began—the term of a pregnancy—I was out of business. My baby was stillborn. The day we closed down I stood in the middle of that restaurant with the staff and screamed so loud you'd have thought I lost my mind. I was broke and in debt to some wonderful people who had invested not so much in the restaurant as in the people who worked there, in their future. One attorney in town had put up $20,000. When the end came he didn't swear at me or make me grovel and feel bad. He just patted me on the back and said I had fought the good fight. I don't know when it will happen, but I'm praying for the day when I can pay him back.

When I meet my maker, I'm not going to ask why I was born black or why I was born poor. I'm going to ask but two things: "Lord, why did you let me marry Wayne Langford, and why did you let me have the Rosebowl restaurant?" Those were two horrible tragedies in my life.

You'd think with a start like that my career as an entrepreneur would be over. But I was determined to make money for these kids and engage them in a successful business. By the time the Rosebowl went belly-up, I had already been selling our sweet potato and white potato pies to two grocery stores—Kroger and Farmer Jack. They committed shelf space to me, and a person I knew who had a restaurant that had closed but still had a valid license to cook let me use the kitchen at night to bake our pies so we could deliver them in the morning.

We made pies for five or six months, but long before that time was up, we realized we were in trouble again. The pies, made from scratch with no preservatives, had no shelf life. We got paid only for pies that were sold. If we brought twelve to the store and ended up selling only four we ended up taking the remainder back, and we sure couldn't eat that many pies ourselves. Unfortunately, there was no pattern to how many pies a store would sell. One day it might be fifteen, while another time we wouldn't sell one for three straight days.

Delivery was also expensive. We would stack up the pies in the back of my old station wagon and deliver pies to all the Kroger and Farmer Jack stores in Washtenaw County and pick up the ones that hadn't sold. My old car burned through gas like you wouldn't believe on those rounds. When we looked at the bottom line it was clear that this little venture was going nowhere, so we abandoned it.

Then in 1989, just as that ill-fated venture was fading from memory, one of our clients came to me with an ad from one of the Detroit papers. It said the Comedy House in Detroit needed comedians.

"You're the biggest comedian we know," he said. "We'd help you come up with some material. They say you could make eight hundred a night if you're good."

Desperate people do desperate things, so several friends sat down and wrote up some jokes. I memorized them and we all headed for the Comedy House and my first performance. I opened by introducing myself as "Rose Martin from Fort Dix, Five Dix, Six Dix, New Jersey." That got a laugh and loosened them up, and I took it from there. Of course, the Comedy House served alcohol and the audience that night had a nice glow to it by the time I took the stage.

But the act must have been good enough because I got a booking at the Comedy Castle, a big-time club in the Detroit suburb of Royal Oak where a lot of famous people started. I opened again with my "Fort Dix, Five Dix..." line and looked out on a sea of expressionless faces just staring back at me—not even a smile in the lot. Suddenly my confidence turned to sheer terror. I searched for my friends Nondi and Bonnie and some of the staff who had come with me, only to find their faces as gloomy as the rest of the audience.

I went on to my second, third, and fourth jokes. Then two drunks at a table on my left started to boo. This audience came to the Comedy Castle all the time. They knew good material, and this wasn't it.

I was never so happy as when I finished my last "joke." I was supposed to leave stage left through a door that opened into the main bar, where I was expected to fraternize with the customers. Instead, I took the side door straight into the alley, where my friends found me. We beat a hasty retreat and my career as a comedian, thank goodness, was behind me.

I HAD ONE LAST ENTREPRENEURIAL EFFORT left in me. In 1995, having either lost my mind or forgotten my past failures, I determined that we could raise some money by going into the jewelry business at a flea market in Ypsilanti. When I got paid that week, I took my check and mailed $600 to my niece in New Jersey, and she went out and bought a pile of costume jewelry.

We rented space at the flea market for $80 a weekend. I went the first day with a few clients from the Center. As we got set up, the man who rented our spot to us pointed out a woman who was breaking down her booth and quitting her own jewelry business. He suggested we shoot over there and make an offer for her display cases. You should have seen the look of amazement when we offered to buy her equipment. I should have looked more carefully at that expression. If I had, I would have seen the look of a person who couldn't escape this flea-bitten market fast enough, and on top of that, some fool comes and offers good money for her setup.

It didn't take long for us to realize that this business lacked one thing. Customers. We would wait there all weekend, see maybe four people, and not sell one pair of earrings. The only way the flea market continued to exist was by luring in new sellers willing to pay the rent to make their little business dream come true. It sure as hell wasn't because there was an abundance of traffic. Needless to say, this venture didn't take long before it, too, was sucking air and rolling belly-up.

Well, truth be told, that wasn't my last effort to find a business that would support us. We tried car washing. Then we tried selling meals we would cook and deliver to people's homes. We put a lot of money and effort into that one and got very little back.

FINALLY, I BELIEVE, I'M WILLING to conclude that I ain't no Bill Gates—that my best efforts are serving people and working one-on-one with potential donors to our Center.

But did I ever tell you the joke about the traveling salesman…

TEN

When Everybody Has Enough

$\mathcal{O}$N THE MID-1980S Cabbage Patch soft-sculpture dolls were all the rage. Every kid in America had to have one of the Cabbage Patch Kids, which came with their own adoption papers. Finding one at Christmas was nearly impossible.

So I was surprised one morning a few weeks before Christmas to arrive at the Peace Neighborhood Center and find a whole batch of those dolls sitting on the steps as donations. It turns out, however, that this generosity wasn't what it seemed. The television news the night before reported that a shipment of counterfeit Cabbage Patch Kids had reached the stores, and to make matters worse, they had been doused in kerosene during shipment to prevent them from being devoured by vermin. Several kids had been injured when the kerosene-soaked dolls got too near an open flame.

Now some generous souls had decided that these counterfeit dolls were too dangerous for their kids but would make wonderful presents for poor children. One guy even had the audacity to leave his name and phone number, so I called him.

"Why would you leave something that would hurt these kids?" I asked. "These kids need protection just like your kids—maybe more. Your kids have dinner every night, a bedtime story, love, an allowance, a family vacation. The kids we deal with here seldom if ever experience these things, so why would you give something that could harm them?"

"I didn't want to waste the ten dollars," he said.

Then there was the woman who came with a big bag of bread that was supposed to be day-old. It must have done a whole lot of aging in that day because the bread was as hard as stone. When I asked her why she'd bring something like that, she said, "I figured some bread is better than no bread."

I explained to her that at the Peace Neighborhood Center we constantly teach the families how wonderful they are, how nobly they've been created. You can't teach kids to value themselves and rejoice in their creation when you are giving them dolls that may explode or bread you can't bite into.

You know the old saying about any shoe is better than no shoe at all? That's bullshit. One of the worst things you can give a poor person is an old pair of worn-out shoes, and yet people offer them to the poor all the time. Shoes adapt to the foot of the wearer, and used shoes can be painful even if they are the right size. And what is the point? You can go to Kmart and get a child a pair of shoes that nobody else has walked in for $10.

When I first came to Ann Arbor, I couldn't understand why so many people who gave us money or volunteered their services would get so uptight when our clients didn't do what the donors expected them to do with the money or help. People who give help with those kinds of expectations are more interested in serving themselves than they are in serving others. I don't think they do it to be mean; I think they are just ignorant of the power of true, unconditional giving.

Take the case of Liz, a bright twenty-year-old woman who lived in public housing. She had a year-old daughter, but wanted very much to enter school at Washtenaw Community College in the fall. Her goal was to complete her basic education at the community college and then transfer to the University of Michigan to get her degree. She wanted to teach dance.

Liz didn't have a car, so two or three days a week she needed someone to pick her and her daughter up early in the morning, drop her daughter at day care, and bring Liz to the college. She could get home by bus. We searched all summer to find someone. Three days before school was to start, we located a woman willing to help. Everyone at the Peace Neighborhood Center was extremely happy because they knew Liz had so much on the ball and was bound to succeed.

The day before Liz's first class the woman volunteer called to say she'd been talking to her friends and they felt Liz was wasting her time studying something that was not a marketable skill—one that would elevate her from her current situation. Therefore this woman volunteer was no longer willing to give up her early morning walks with her well-to-do neighbors to help this young woman.

I was deeply disappointed. I'm always trying to get people to give more than money because when they give something of themselves the changes are more permanent. When people get personally involved, the walls of ignorance begin to crumble.

I'm happy to say, however, that the woman who turned down Liz has become my best friend, and she is one of the most generous people in the world. But it was a struggle for her to break out of the uptight mentality of her upper-class neighbors. They fought her every time she took a step toward understanding, sharing. But she did it, and as in so many cases, the transformation came without warning. Her growth paid off not only in the help she gave the community but in the insights she gained in raising her own children.

I see it all the time—people who want to serve themselves, not the true needs of others. This is one of the attitudes toward giving that tortures my soul.

I came to the Center one Monday morning at eight o'clock, opened the door, and there was a man waiting for me.

"Ms. Martin, my daughter got married on Saturday. We invited two hundred people and only ninety showed. I have salad here for one hundred ten people, and I didn't want to throw it out. I wanted to make sure it got used, and I thought you might want to give it to the folks who come here."

"Was it refrigerated?" I asked.

"Sort of," he said.

"Has it got dressing on it?"

"They put house dressing on it," he said.

You can imagine what condition this salad was in.

People come to the Center at Christmas with bags and bags of toys to give away, but they are things they want to buy rather than things the people in need want.

Other people come to me and tell me they'd like to help a family, so we provide them a list of things various families have said they want to have for Christmas. Which invariably leads people to argue with me.

"Why would he want a Game Boy Color when he's living in public housing?"

"I don't pay one hundred dollars for a jacket for my kid; I'm not going to pay seventy-five bucks for theirs."

People understand that free choice and decision making are a fundamental part of our society. They count on it, but somehow when it comes to poor people, choice doesn't matter. My philosophy is that the only way to help people become part of the solution and not part of the problem is to put choice in their hands. Poverty doesn't change that.

Once you give to someone, you can't follow that money into the bank or into the mouth of the person you're serving. If you believe in blessings, if you believe in sharing, you don't have to bird-dog those you share with. I tell people who are giving that if they are spiritually mature enough to see the benefit of sharing what they have with other people, they will receive any positive karma coming their way regardless of what the person does with their gift.

People also think poor folks want something for nothing. In truth, most people want *less* than we are willing to give them. To discover what people really need, we have to take the time to listen, because often the people we're trying to help don't speak with the clarity and assurance that the rest of us speak with. But if you listen carefully, you'll find out what their needs and wants are.

Mrs. Betty Prince came to my office one day with all eight of her kids. Her husband worked for the city of Ann Arbor, and he had gotten hurt and was unable to work. There was a technicality that prevented his benefits from kicking in right away.

Betty and her eight little children needed something to eat. We checked out her story and it was true, so I gave her $200 worth of food certificates for a local grocery store. Most people would think that was too much. The haves want to give you just enough so you keep coming back, but not enough that you're no longer in need. That's one thing, among many, that's wrong with welfare; they give you just enough to keep you coming back.

When I came out of my office at four o'clock in the afternoon, I discovered Mrs. Prince and her kids were still there.

"Is there a problem?" I asked.

"Sort of," she said.

"I expected that you would have bought groceries and been home by now preparing dinner for your family," I said.

She explained to me that she had no way of getting groceries home from the store. So why, I asked her, didn't she say something to me six hours ago? I would have given her a ride or a cab voucher.

"You already gave me two hundred dollars for food," she said. "I couldn't ask you for a way to get home." So she just camped out there all day, trying to think of a way to get herself and her eight kids to the grocery store and then get $200 worth of groceries home. In the end, all she wanted was a ride home.

The next time we heard from Mrs. Prince was seven or eight years later. She was getting her GED from the adult education program and planned to enroll at Washtenaw Community College and then go on to Eastern Michigan University to become a physical therapist.

We decided to do something special for her, so I asked her what she would like as a gift.

"I've always wanted to ride in a limousine," she told me. So I went to some of our wealthy supporters and said I had a mother of eight children who was getting her GED and had made a request of me that would cost $279. I didn't tell them about the limousine because I knew they would have thought it was a waste of money, and I was too busy providing services to take two days to explain it to them.

One reason we are what we are at Peace Neighborhood Center is that when the people we serve move on to a better life, they come back and help us. They don't necessarily give us money, but if a family is evicted, they give them a place to stay or feed them or provide transportation. Or they work in recovery groups to teach parents how to be more affectionate with their children. Or they teach fathers how to spend money wisely on their families and not in bars or on whores.

That's why during the holidays we don't allow people of means to come in and serve the homeless and the have-nots. "We give you a lot of money," they'll say, "so why can't we come at Christmas time and serve?"

Because, I tell them, it works so well to have people who were once in need themselves serving the food and providing small talk. It works like a charm to have someone who is serving meals sit down and say, "Ten years ago I was exactly where you are. I am now a graduate of the University of Michigan, I have a teaching certificate, I'm reunited with my children."

"I was where you are now when I came to this place," they will say, "and these are the people who have stuck by me. You can't expect me to take care of you, but I can help you get on your own way."

This is not just black folks or white folks. This is people helping people.

The other attitude toward giving that drives me crazy is the belief that poverty is so widespread we can't do anything to change it. Nonsense. If there are a thousand people who are hungry and you can't feed but one, feed that one. Don't hide behind the enormity of the problem. Yes, over 30 million people in this country live below the poverty line. But don't let that be your excuse to run from the problem and become totally self-centered. It's true that the poor are always with us, but they don't have to be *that* poor.

Speaking of excuses not to help people, I once had an audience with one of Ann Arbor's wealthiest and most influential men. I had to eat shit and run with the dogs to get to see him, but I finally got an appointment and gave him my spiel on the Peace Neighborhood Center.

"Ms. Martin," he said when I was done, "if you will tell me why people have children and know they can't feed them, if you can make me understand that, I will give you whatever you want."

The question shocked me, but it was a courageous question — one I'm sure 90 percent of the people who give me money have tucked away somewhere in the back of their mind.

"If you promise me you won't be offended," I said, "I'll tell you why."

"Of course. I've been trying to learn this for years."

"Because they will never own anything like all the money and possessions you and all the other wealthy people have. Children give them great pleasure, just as you look at your bank statement or your material possessions and feel a sense of satisfaction. Children belong to them; they give them positive self-esteem.

Childbearing is something they can do that you can't stop them from doing.

"Poor people have children because they feel the need," I continued, "because they feel a great sense of accomplishment, and having children is something they can do well. It's something wealthy folks can't fuck them out of. They don't have kids assuming they won't be able to feed them. They have children with a sense of hope. It's only afterwards they have to face the awful reality of not being able to care for them."

This rich businessman eventually contributed a small amount to the Center—$250 as I remember. I suspect my answer was not what he wanted to hear, but I give him credit for having the balls to ask.

I had even less luck with another business magnate—Tom Monaghan, founder of Domino's Pizza. Sometimes my enthusiasm for providing services to people in need is so great I just assume that others will see the same needs and respond in the same way.

His neighbors at Domino's Farms, the company's headquarters at the outskirts of Ann Arbor, were angry when he installed a massive display of Christmas lights and illuminated religious decorations. The lights became a magnet that attracted people from all over the area, and the residents of the neighborhood were beside themselves when tens of thousands of cars came to drive by the display. They took Monaghan to court and—temporarily, it turned out—got the lights turned off.

In 1988, when the newspaper reported that it was lights out at Domino's Farms, I got the idea—brilliant,

I thought—that Mr. Monaghan, who was a recognized philanthropist in the community, might be willing to light up the eyes of some children at the Peace Neighborhood Center. So I loaded a hundred kids from the projects on two buses and we drove out to Domino's Farms. I hoped that Mr. Monaghan might be delighted to contribute to these kids who would not have Christmas unless someone played Santa Claus for them. We created a banner that read "Dear Mr. Monaghan, please make us your Christmas lights this year."

We didn't have an appointment, but when we arrived in the lobby, Mr. Monaghan's assistant got ahold of him and he came out and spoke with us. I explained a little about Peace Neighborhood Center. There are so many similarities between my life and Mr. Monaghan's that I thought we'd have a lot to talk about. He was an orphan like I was. He always dreamed of owning a ball team. I always dreamed of owning a business that could finance the kind of services I want to provide. I had foster parents. He had foster parents. I thought we'd be great pals, make a great team.

Not so, apparently. It was not long after that a United Way representative paid me a visit. We had been struggling for some time to get recognition as a United Way participating agency and had the support of several powerful people in town who knew about our work. The United Way spokesperson told me, gently but firmly, that if I were ever to embarrass Mr.

Monaghan again I could forget about ever getting money from the agency.

It appeared my priorities for giving and sharing were not quite the same as Mr. Monaghan's, although the donations to his St. Nicholas Light Display have since been used to benefit a large number of children's charities—and we eventually received $500.

There are people in the black community who call me the ADCP (Aid to Dependent Children Police) because I don't think it's right that money meant to feed little kids is being used for every damn thing but feeding those kids.

In the late 1980s a woman I knew was being evicted. She was on a HUD housing subsidy and was paying $28 a month rent but was still four or five months behind. She had five kids and was giving her food stamps to three dope boys who were using a house out in Pine Lake as a distribution point for drugs. I was determined those food stamps would go to the children who needed them, not the drug dealers.

In the Peace Neighborhood Center programs we always have at least a half dozen people we've helped get off drugs and who have been clean for many years. All of them told me not to go near this house.

"We know what you used to do years ago," one of them said, "and you got away with it. But things have changed. You can't do it now. These young boys will kill you."

I checked with my friend Blondeen Munson at

legal aid and she said, "I *know* you ain't going up in there."

But I was. When I ran up to the dope house I immediately realized it was the wrong thing to do—my advisers were right. Usually, when I went into a dope house there were two or three people in there who knew me and appreciated my role in the community. These guys, however, were from Detroit. They not only didn't know me, they had guns and you could tell by the look in their eyes they didn't much care whether I lived or died. I'll admit I was scared.

Stepping inside, I was shocked to see food stamps scattered all over the table—you would have thought it was a subsidiary of the Department of Agriculture. When I saw all those food stamps that had been exchanged for drugs, my fear disappeared and I started raising hell.

"What the hell is going on?" I shouted. "Do you know how many little kids are not going to eat today?"

By now, three or four people had come out of their homes surrounding the dope house and they were calling in, "Ms. Rose, you all right?" "Ms. Rose, do you want me to call the police?"

The dope boys didn't want attention drawn to the house, so this one little guy—he couldn't have been more than eighteen—said, "Give the bitch the stamps she came after." They brushed the stamps off the table, scattering them on the floor. I bent down and scraped them up—about $300 worth—and beat a fast retreat.

Often the people who need our gifts the most are the ones that may seem the least deserving. I like giving to those people.

One woman I had contact with over the years was continually trying to manipulate the Peace Neighborhood Center's programs to simply advance her drug habit. I wouldn't let her lie about her situation and use the Center's programs that way. And I told her so to her face.

She had lots of kids, many of whom used Peace's youth programs daily, and she was unemployed and on welfare. For twenty years she would roll her eyes at me every time she saw me, and often shout obscenities at me. She used any informal gathering around the courtyard where she lived as a forum to lie about me, call me unfair, even claim I was some kind of Satan.

After her twenty-two-year-old daughter died of a drug overdose, Thelma Lea was evicted from her home and her other children were taken into custody by the state. She ended up living behind a Dumpster in Ypsilanti, Michigan.

A client of mine in drug recovery brought Thelma Lea's situation to my attention. After several restless nights—in which I saw Thelma Lea's face in my dreams even though I hadn't seen her in person for years—I knew I couldn't resist trying to help her. I found her, offered her a room in my home, and fed her daily and nursed her back to health. She stayed with me for some two months, and eventually I was able to talk her into going to a treatment center for substance abuse.

While she was with me, she had trouble understanding why I had taken her in. The first few days she just cried and cried. "You didn't have to take me in," she said. "You could have let me die."

"But you are alive," I told her, "and when you are at the bottom of the barrel there is nowhere left to go but up. God has shown me no limits to His love, so why should I limit my love to you or anyone else."

I TAKE HEART THAT THERE ARE PEOPLE who know how to give, who do it unconditionally, and who are willing to do so over and over again. There are half a dozen people in this city that I can go to in extreme cases and ask them for anything, small or large, to assist another human being. And they have never turned me down.

Bob and Martha Seward are among them. They are folks who will come to me and say, "Don't explain the details of what you're trying to do; just tell me what you need."

The first time they approached me was before Christmas. They had decided their family was not going to buy gifts for each other; they were going to help people who didn't have anything.

It was during the Cabbage Patch doll frenzy I mentioned earlier, and kids were just beside themselves to have one.

"Find me thirty Cabbage Patch dolls that won't ignite," I told them; I didn't mention that I had received plenty of the kerosene-soaked ones on our doorstep. They proceeded to scour southeastern Michigan for the dolls, spending two whole days and nights on the road. They drove to Detroit and Toledo, Ohio. Every time they scored a few more dolls, they'd call me and report, "We've got eight," "We've got ten more." At $30–$35 apiece they weren't cheap, but the Sewards never flagged in their enthusiasm. I think it made as exciting a Christmas for them as it did for the kids who got the dolls.

Another woman—a wonderful person who's helped me many times—gave me $500 without question to help a man who was in a horrible situation. But afterward she asked, "When do you stop?"

"When it's even," I said. "When everybody has enough—not everything they want, but what they truly need."

ONE ROSE BLOOMING

ELEVEN

Bridging the Gap

𝒜 SINGLE PICTURE ON THE FRONT PAGE of the *Ann Arbor News* told the story best. There had been a winter storm, and, like all the other streets in town, North Maple Road had turned into a sheet of ice. In the picture, the white folks who lived in homes on one side of North Maple were reaching out to the black people coming out of the housing projects on the other side of the road to keep them from slipping and falling as they crossed the street.

The picture wasn't staged. And it said everything about a program called Project Change that in the mid-1970s brought white people and black people together to solve problems and share friendships.

Every now and then government and people get together in good faith to create something that shows just how good life on this earth could be if we tried a little harder, reached out a bit more, gave something of our souls to each other. Project Change was a shining example of what we can do when we put our hearts to it.

It began in 1974 when the city of Ann Arbor and the Housing Commission decided to do something to enhance the lives of people living in public housing. Ann Arbor has long had a scattered-site concept for its public housing, which means that public housing is distributed throughout the city rather than concentrated in one area.

One of the first public housing sites created under this concept was North Maple Village (now North Maple Estates), built on the outskirts of the city. There were problems from the start. Many of the white folks who lived around the site opposed it entirely; they were afraid their property values would decline. Others objected to the city putting people in public housing in their community without providing the low-income families who lived there with the services they needed.

To solve these problems, the city came up with Project Change, and they hired a sharp social worker named Sally Vinter to run it. She was to work with me on the program since I then worked for the Housing Commission and had the trust of the people in the projects.

Project Change gave birth to many innovative programs that brought people together. At the program's core was a meeting once or twice a week between the folks who owned homes around the North Maple public housing and the residents of the project. The meetings would take place either in a homeowner's residence or in the project.

Another method for breaking down ignorance and prejudice on both sides was what we called "coffee sips." Every Wednesday we would invite people like the mayor, city council members, and school officials to come into the neighborhood and talk about issues of importance to our neighborhood. It was not unusual to walk into a coffee sip and see the lieutenant governor or some other high-ranking official talking to people, trying to find out how to change things, how to bring resources to the community.

Many of the people living in the project and those with homes near it shared one thing: they were parents. And the care of children was one of the most important topics to them, and one of the first topics to be addressed.

Early in those meetings, for example, the homeowners wanted to know why their kids were getting their asses kicked every day by the kids in public housing.

Vicki DeNardi was one of them. Her son, Todd, was a fourth-grader at the time, and every day for two years boys from the North Maple project had harassed him on his way to Haisley School. Todd was one of the smallest kids in his class, and to make matters worse, he wasn't very fast. As a result, he was getting more than his share of abuse.

Someone suggested we invite the boys who were harassing Todd to accompany their mothers to the next coffee sip at Vicki's house. We all gathered in the living room on the chosen day and were making small talk, getting ready for the coffee sip to start formally, when Todd arrived with his dad. When Todd saw the boys who had been attacking him sitting in his living room, he let out a scream of terror. He was only seven or eight, but you could see what he was thinking: These kids can get in my house now; there's no place safe. Why the hell would my parents welcome these barbarians into my safe space?

Todd started hyperventilating and his cheeks turned red as cherries. But his mother took his hand and guided him to the sofa where the other boys were sitting with their mothers.

"Okay, Todd," I said, "what's been happening, and what would you like to see changed?"

I told him all the people in the room would be supportive because we were trying to demonstrate that everyone has a right to exist and lead their lives without being beaten up by anyone else. We are all neighbors and we are all listening because we want it to stop, I told him.

"When was the last time they jumped you?" I asked.

"Yesterday."

"That's the last time you'll be jumped on," I said. "I give you my word."

As we talked it became clear that the boys who lived in the North Maple project had no idea that Todd was messed up so severely by what they were doing. They got their asses kicked every day by somebody, and they were just passing on the favor. It was like water off a duck's back to them, but Todd wasn't being brought up in that kind of environment. To him it was traumatic.

Once the other boys understood how it was affecting Todd, they agreed not to harass him any more. They came up with the idea; we didn't.

Two days later, Sally Vinter and I were watching the kids walking to school. And there was little Todd sharing the sandwich from his lunch with one of the boys who had picked on him.

Three or four months later, I was called to the school by some of the kids from the North Maple project because a new group of kids—kids from outside the project—had been bothering Todd. Protecting Todd, the kids from the project were whaling on Todd's new tormentors. Todd not only had new friends, he had his own security guard.

Not long ago, I was coming out of the grocery store with Damon, one of the boys who had harassed Todd. Now, of course, Damon was a grown man. As we stepped out of the store, there almost in front of him—after all those years—was Todd. They sprinted across the parking lot toward each other, screaming out a greeting you could hear all the way to Detroit. Todd picked Damon up with a big bear hug and before long they were exchanging phone numbers. By then, people coming out of the store were looking at them wondering what the story was. I wish I could have told them.

At one of the coffee sips, Ellie, a black woman, shared how much she would love to talk to her son's teacher. She was fearful of talking with her because the teacher was always patronizing her, patting her on the shoulder to avoid having to deal with her.

Two white woman at the coffee sip, who had no problem getting heard by the teachers, told Ellie they would go down to the school with her and demand the teacher give her the respect and attention she deserved.

Ellie said the teacher's whole attitude changed after that. Suddenly the teacher had time for her, and Ellie was able to express her concerns in a way that she hadn't been able to do when her six older children went through the same class.

Gradually, but dramatically, the prejudice and ignorance between the people living outside the housing project, who were largely white, and the low-income people in the project, who were predominantly black, began to fade. Some of the white neighbors shared with the group that they were taking flak from their friends for even coming into the projects. Hadn't they read in the paper that a pizza driver had been robbed and a cab driver beaten up?

The folks in the project were taking their own abuse. Why would they want friendships with these white folks who had done so much to keep them down for generations? If the whites really cared, some folks in the project said, why didn't they do something to improve the black people's financial well-being.

But the talking continued, and the old attitudes began to melt away. You couldn't bullshit at those coffee sips. You had thirty or forty people in the room calling you out. People had to face who they were, and they had to deal with the problem in front of them.

I believe there was even more prejudice on the part of the black people who lived in the project at the beginning. They knew that the people who owned the homes around the project had fought the city when it wanted to build public housing there. But they came to understand that, in part, it wasn't because the homeowners didn't want black people or poor people to live there; it was because they wanted poor people to have the services they needed to maintain themselves in the community.

You could understand their concern by just looking at how shabbily that project was built. The families at North Maple Village would keep a mop and a bucket at the back door to clean up the dirt because there were no proper sidewalks.

Although the homes were only two or three years old when Project Change started, there were cracks in the molding around the doors and windows that made some of the living rooms so drafty that it was almost like sitting outside. And if they weren't so drafty you couldn't stand it, they were super hot. If you ran water in the bathtub, you could count on your neighbor hearing it several doors down.

Many of the homeowners who came to the meetings worked in local companies and offered jobs to the people from the project, giving them a chance they would never have had otherwise. Many of the well-to-do women gave business suits and nice clothes to women in the project so they would look good when they went out to apply for jobs. People exchanged information about employment and resources.

In return, the white homeowners were invited to social gatherings that families in the project had, so they could understand how the people who lived—literally—on the other side of the road experienced life.

Just to show you how close these groups became, the Project Change participants in the project laid down the law to their neighbors: everyone who came into the project would leave with all their belongings. Theft would not be tolerated. Young people, mainly between fourteen and twenty years old, served as guards and watched the visitors' cars to make sure that nothing was taken while they were at the housing project.

By the same token, when the Housing Commission wanted to raise the rents at the project, the people who lived across the street—now fully aware of the conditions their neighbors were living under—got together with the North Maple project residents and fought against the rent increases.

The Project Change folks also bought paint and construction materials at neighborhood stores and refurbished all of the project homes.

At one coffee sip, an affluent white woman broke down and began to cry uncontrollably as we were discussing how to support each other as parents. When asked what was wrong, she blurted out, "Don't walk, Nikki!" She was referring to a baby who belonged to one of the North Maple mothers and was so adored by everyone she had become a kind of mascot for the group.

As the group gathered around her to offer comfort, she explained: "I've noticed that the babies of the mothers here at North Maple are loved and cared for greatly as long as they are too young to walk. The moment they start walking, the babies are left pretty much to take care of themselves. It frightens me to death to think of that happening to our Nikki."

Nikki was pulling herself up on her baby carrier in the middle of the room. The woman became so excited she got up from her chair and ran over to Nikki, dropped to her knees in front of the baby carrier, and began to weep again. "I don't understand why more of your children aren't hurt or killed the way you leave them at such a young age to fend for themselves," she cried.

By this time, every white woman in the room was nodding in agreement. They understood what she meant. And so did some of the North Maple parents. But not all of them.

"You got your nerve making those statements in here," one of the black mothers said. "You have the time and money to be what you need to be for your children. We don't. Most of us have to scrape like hell every day just to pay the rent and put food on the table."

The silence in the room was deafening. We ended the meeting that day in silence, but what a meeting it was! We had a chance to look into each other's lives in a way we hadn't before, and in the process we were becoming better friends.

We were having a problem with the police harassing people as they entered the project in their cars. We asked Harold Olson, the deputy chief of police at the time, to come to the coffee sip and discuss the issue. It was easy to get his attention since for many years elections in Ann Arbor were so close that a group of forty people in the same room would get a prospective candidate's attention. Also at the time, we were getting black people registered to vote who had never voted before. Chief Olson investigated the problem and the harassment stopped.

The lines of communication between the police department and the poor people in that housing project opened up phenomenally. One day some kids from North Maple went down to the Kmart half a block away and stole ten bikes off a tractor-trailer as it was being unloaded.

Both Kmart and the police called me. I got some kids together, white and black, from that neighborhood, and we went looking for the kids who stole the bikes. My posse and I located one of the bike thieves, and I went into his house and asked him why he had stolen the bike.

"That bike is not yours," I said.

"Yes it is."

"How is it your bike? You didn't pay for it. You stole it off a truck in front of Kmart."

"You know how heavy a bike in a box is?" he said. "I ran all the way down here from Kmart with that bike on my back. It's mine!" He let me know in no uncertain terms what he went through to get the bike. In his mind, that was how he earned it.

He said all of this in front of his mother, and she did not correct him. In fact, she asked me who I thought I was, the police? She called me Aunt Jemima and a whole lot of other names to try to embarrass me, but I was trying to show the kids who were on board with Project Change that if you did things right, you would get rewards for your behavior.

"Allan, you didn't pay for the bike," I told him. "I don't care if you ran from the next town with it. We're trying to change things in this neighborhood."

With the help of some of his peers—his road buddies who were now active in Project Change—we were able to locate the bike, and we talked with other kids who told us where the rest of the bikes were.

Six or seven of those bikes were in the house of a thirteen-year-old boy whose mother would take $20 a day from him to play bingo. Of course, he didn't have a job, but she never questioned that the money was coming from stolen goods and drug sales.

She made me so damn mad I decided to get back at her. I told her son, Steve, that I wanted him to come talk with me the next Wednesday. He came to my office, and we went for a walk.

"Steve, you know how busy I am," I said. "I have very little time, but this is so important because you are so smart. I'm taking this time to talk with you because you are just so bright."

"What do you mean 'bright'?" he asked. "I'm flunking out of school."

"You're spiritually bright," I told him. "The academics you will get."

I could see he was thinking about this.

"Do you believe there's a power in this universe greater than any of us?" I asked.

"Sure," he said. "God."

"When you're selling drugs and stolen property to folks, you're taking God's place with them because you aren't showing them how to stay on a straight path, a righteous path, an honest path. You are making those people dependent on you. You're giving them tunnel vision to set their sights on you, and you're nothing but a mortal human being. Should they be looking for Steve or should they be looking for God?"

He thought about that for a minute. "You know," he said, "I don't mind fucking with anybody else, but the last person I want to fuck with is God."

That's how his mother got paid back. I educated her son spiritually. I didn't fight him. I didn't argue with him. I didn't preach hell and damnation. I just appealed to Steve's heart.

Project Change went on for three or four years. And it lived up to its name on many accounts. We were able to find better housing for some people who lived there. The number of out-of-wedlock births dropped significantly. We started a drop-in center, and parents who had to go shopping or go to the doctor or to school for a teacher conference could drop their children off there or with a neighbor who lived across the street from the project.

We had a lot of barbecues on Friday nights where all the families got together, drank, danced, and talked openly and honestly about their prejudices without anybody getting pissed off or starting a fight.

The haves understood why the have-nots felt the way they did, and the have-nots began to understand why the haves behaved the way they did. When either group needed something neither one had, they got together and looked for it.

But then the politics changed and resources dried up. Project Change was no longer a priority of the mayor and the city council. By then they had rehabilitated the cosmetics of the housing project and people thought because the buildings looked better that all the healing had been done. They assumed four hundred years of illness vanished with a few strokes of a paintbrush.

Like too many programs in our society, when something begins to work, we get rid of it. If the problem isn't new or festering, we ignore it until it erupts once again. One of the reasons we keep reinventing the wheel in social services is that there's no money to keep doing the things that work.

TWELVE

Not Making the Grade

I T HAS BEEN NEARLY HALF A CENTURY since the Supreme Court ruled in *Brown v. Board of Education* that schools in this country must be integrated, that "separate but equal" schools were unconstitutional. Most Americans today seem to confidently assume that our current integrated school systems are providing equal educational opportunities for both black and white children—that we are living up to the American dream of equal education for all.

My experience with kids in schools has proved to me time and again that it just isn't so. Although the school system where I work is lauded for its progressive programs and was one of the earliest northern systems to integrate, the simple fact is that kids who are poor and black don't get the same educational opportunities that other kids do.

It's not a matter of putting black and white bodies in the same schoolroom. It's a matter of attitude. And the situation will not improve until everyone—parents, kids, teachers, administrators, and people in the community who ought to care about the schools even if they don't have kids in them—make it their business to be involved in the schools.

Sometimes the unequal treatment of minorities is blatantly obvious. Sometimes it is subtle, so subtle even teachers don't realize what they are doing.

Take the case of Ricky. Ricky had lived with his mother the first eight years of his life, and by the time he was nine he was living with me as his guardian because his mother was sick with emotional problems. He was having trouble adjusting to Dicken School, and I kept running over there to talk with him and his teachers.

In my early days as a service provider, I did things differently; it was nothing for me to kick someone's ass if they got into trouble. That's not my thing anymore, but back then it was. The teacher kept telling me that Ricky was misbehaving, and I kept punishing him. Then one day Ricky mouthed off to his teacher and got sent home. That night I heard him in his room crying. I had worked fourteen hours, and I was dead tired. The last thing I wanted was a nine-year-old crying.

"Ricky, what is it?" I asked him.

"Everybody told you all the things I did today, and I did do those things, but not before the teacher kicked the chair out from under me. The teacher kept asking me to settle down, and I didn't. When I tried to sit down, he kicked the chair out from under me and I hit the floor. The whole class laughed."

When I went to the school I heard all about Ricky's misdeeds from the principal, the teacher, and the teacher's aide. Nobody bothered to mention what the teacher did to Ricky. An already angry kid suddenly became angrier. Predictably, he lit into the teacher and got suspended.

That's not teaching. That's not guidance. That's provocation. And you can bet that kind of provocation was not happening to the well-to-do kids in school.

Some kids came to me in the mid-1970s and one said, "Rose, Miss Josie won't call on Shorty. He waves his hand all the time, and she passes over him and never calls on him."

So I went down to see Miss Josie at Slauson Junior High, where Shorty was a seventh-grader. Do you know what she said to me? She said, "Miss Martin, I spend a lot of time trying to make a point in a classroom of thirty children, and the last thing I want to do is call on someone, at a very vital point in my teaching, who may give me the wrong answer. I want to call on a kid who's sure to give me the right answer so I can get my point across."

Now you don't have to be a Doctor of Educational Theory to figure out who is getting educated here and who is not.

"How do you think Shorty feels being passed over?" I asked the teacher. "It takes a lot of nerve for him to raise his hand in the first place because he's in a class with a lot of wealthy kids. I would call on him for no other reason than because he has the balls to raise his hand. He's outnumbered financially, educationally, and in life experience. He's not going home to a warm home and dinner. He has a mother who's been on welfare all her life and is addicted to alcohol. He's going home to arguments and fights. Raising his hand in your class is an act of courage."

She just looked at me like I was from another galaxy.

But you can't apply the same rules to kids who come from homes dominated by poverty, drugs, abuse, and all the other atrocities that the underclass experiences. When you have kids experiencing that kind of trauma rubbing elbows with kids from privileged, well-to-do homes, the educational playing field is not even. The integration that in theory should help the black kids instead works to their disadvantage.

And the involvement of parents plays a large part in it, as well. The parents of the prosperous kids come to school often, check curriculums, and get involved in activities and projects that go on in the classroom. The teachers see them as comrades who lend a helping hand.

The poor kids' parents often aren't there. Should they be? Of course. But too often they feel as out of place as their kids. Or they are putting every bit of energy they have into providing food and shelter for their family. Or they are strung out on drugs and completely unresponsive to their kids' education.

Whatever the cause, we can't educate these young people unless we take into consideration their backgrounds, the baggage they bring to school every day. Just putting whites and blacks in the same classroom does little, if anything, to solve the problem.

How are you going to educate a twelve-year-old girl like Annie if you don't factor in her background? She came to me in the mid-1980s at the Peace Neighborhood Center because she was pregnant. That doesn't happen often, I'm happy to say, because we are very good at educating kids on how to protect themselves sexually.

We have a club called Rose's Good Girl Friends, and one rule is that the only person you can ever tell what we talk about in the club is your momma. Otherwise, you don't tell a soul. I try to teach these young girls the way I taught my kids—to give them a safe place to talk about what is on their minds.

But Annie was seven months pregnant and she didn't know why. A variety of health officials were there to help her, and they even arranged for a visit by a doctor from California who had a reputation for being successful in delivering babies from mothers whose bodies weren't developed enough to cooperate with childbirth.

Annie had been one of the kids in Rose's Good Girl Friends and I was puzzled why she had let herself get pregnant—and especially that she didn't seem to know how she got that way.

"You don't know how you got pregnant?" I asked.

"Good girl friend," she said, "don't you have to have a boyfriend to be pregnant?"

I knew her well enough to know she wouldn't lie about not having a boyfriend. And after much talk and a little investigation I was able to put the pieces together. Annie's mother had brought one of her drug pals home with her and in the middle of the night that man had laid down with this young child. It was so horrific to her that she blotted it totally out of her mind and had no way of relating it to her pregnant condition.

Now imagine for a moment that Annie's in the classroom sometime after experiencing this unspeakable assault. She seems distant, uninterested. Is she stupid? Hostile? Why is she so reluctant to raise her hand and answer questions? Does her education seem like a lost cause to the teacher?

The simple fact is that you can't possibly educate this child unless you make an effort—and it may take a hell of an effort—to understand her and her background. Just because she's sitting next to wealthy kids isn't going to help, and in fact may make things even more difficult for her.

There is a lot we can do to make education work for these kids. For one thing, we need those kids and parents whom God has smiled on to take up the cause for those disadvantaged kids and act as guardian angels for them. We need parents who know how to influence the school system to be there for the kids whose parents are unable to fight for them.

What we don't need are asinine rules and regulations that cause the have-not kids to suffer even more. Many times in my thirty years of experience I have seen children suspended from school because some parent who aligned herself with the teachers and administration in that school had ordered it. Parents of the have-not kids go into the same arena feeling beaten, and half the time they don't even show up because they feel there is nothing they could say that would give them equal footing.

But understanding where kids are coming from is not the only answer to providing quality education for everyone. We—teachers, administrators, and the community—need to raise our expectations.

A kid named Rona came into Peace Neighborhood Center one day, waving her report card, happy as a lark because she got a D in math.

"Why are you so happy with this damn D?" I asked.

"My teacher said it was good," she said. "Yes, he did."

I jumped over my desk and shot down to that schoolhouse, do you hear me, and I caught the teacher coming out of class. My jaws were so tight my drawers weren't touching me anywhere.

"Can Rona get into college with this report card?" I asked.

"Oh, no, no," he said.

"Then why in the world would you tell her this is good?"

His explanation went like this: "I knew the deficiencies in her family, that she didn't have anyone at home to help her, that doing well in school is not a priority. I thought the fact that she didn't fail and got a D should be praised."

He had a point. He was thinking, in some ways, like I have proposed all teachers should think. But it wasn't good enough for me.

"Why not say that you didn't fail and that's good but you have to do better?" I asked. "Why make her feel that this is as good as she can do?"

Later, I told Rona that she was correct that this was better than failing, but she would never do any of the things she told me she wanted to do with Ds on her report card. The next year Rona ended up coming to our home to live, and she got all Bs and Cs for two years.

And after I went off on him, that teacher and I actually became good friends. In fact, he visited me often at the Peace Neighborhood Center and plagued me to teach him how to communicate with kids like Rona. He wanted to know how to make education work for kids like her.

And one of those ways is not to let children like her settle for a poor report card. That's a nice way teachers have of saying, "You'll never amount to much; you're all you are going to be."

I tell kids "Don't bring me 'needs improvement.' I want to see 'satisfactory.' I want to see As and Bs."

Cities and school boards spend tens of thousands of dollars to figure out ways to get kids from public housing to go to school. But no plan will work unless the kids see that school is an investment that has a payoff for them. Too often there is no one at home motivating them, getting involved in school projects, and pointing out how education leads to a better life. Too many parents of the poor kids are more worried about putting food on the table and clothes on their kids.

In the late 1980s kids from the North Maple project who attended Forsythe Junior High were getting into trouble with the central administration because the absentee rate was so high.

One day I went to one of my guardian angels and asked for some money. I took the check and went to the bank and got some ones, fives, tens, and twenties and put them in a paper bag. The next morning I showed up at the bus stop and started going into my bag and handing out money to the children there.

"This is for going to school this morning," I told them. "This is just a little incentive, not a payment for going to school."

After that, I would occasionally show up with money. The attendance rate improved dramatically. Sometimes it just takes a little imagination, not gobs of money, to make the point. These kids were not children who receive an allowance or other monetary rewards like some of their counterparts.

Sometimes solutions are simple. In 1994 kids from the housing project who rode the bus to Dicken Elementary School were wreaking havoc — getting into fights and causing all kinds of problems. The teachers and administrators didn't know what to do about the situation since they couldn't expel all sixty kids who rode the bus without incurring the wrath of the community.

I went to a few of my guardian angels and asked if they would give me $200 each. I ended up with $1,000. I took the money to the grocery store and bought food, and then I talked the grannies in the neighborhood into fixing breakfast for the kids who were causing the trouble on the bus. Once we fed them, the fights stopped.

I still have a letter from the former principal of Dicken Elementary School asking me how I knew that food was the answer to the problem. That's easy. I can still remember going to school hungry, and when I was hungry, I wanted to kick everyone's ass, too.

Since that time we've had a breakfast program every morning for kids in elementary school. They can get juice or pancakes or cereal before they go to school in the morning. Some kids still have inept parents or families that are apathetic about education. Some kids still have parents who are unemployed or abusing drugs. But at least these kids are doing better because they stop by a granny's house in the morning not only for food but a taste of love, as well.

We need to be constantly thinking of new ways to get inside the psyche of kids who are having difficulty relating to school. We need to motivate them, encourage them, and give them positive experiences. And when those kids don't get positive encouragement at home, all of us — from the parents of the affluent to the school administrators — need to take up their cause.

Maybe then we will begin to realize the equal education that was promised us nearly fifty years ago. Maybe then we won't keep kicking the chair out from under the kids who can least handle it.

THIRTEEN

Coping with Cops

*J*UST LIKE TEACHERS, police officers need to look at their job with a more spiritual eye.

Sure, they have a tough and dangerous job, and there are many occasions when they need to be the hard-ass enforcers that protect our society. But I can tell you from a lifetime of dealing with the cops—and much of it in a liberal, supposedly progressive town, at that—that police are too often rude and arrogant to minorities. There are far too many times when they could help heal a wounded community, but instead simply add to the abuse.

It doesn't make me happy to have this attitude toward the police in Ann Arbor, but it is based on many ugly experiences. And bear in mind, I have two sons and a daughter-in-law who are or have been police officers, and I'm extremely proud of them. But I've also seen from the inside how these departments operate.

Minorities, poor people, and people with little power know they are targeted by police. And it hurts them and eats away any hope they have of being treated fairly and humanely. It divides people when we should be bringing them together to help each other.

A couple of years back, my friend Percy told me he'd been having nightmares for a month about an incident he'd witnessed. He was still upset and disoriented by it.

As Percy was coming out of a store one night, he saw some white boys beating up an old white woman. Percy's instinct was to rush over and start kicking ass to protect the woman. But he didn't lift a hand to help, going on about his business as though the whole thing never happened. Doing nothing bothered him greatly.

"Why didn't you help?" I asked him.

"Because the police would have come," Percy said, "and I'd be in trouble because I'm a black male, poor, and an ex-con."

I assured him that I knew he was not the kind of person to walk away voluntarily.

"It's hard for me to live with myself," he said. "But I know what the system is like. The minute they put me in their computer and saw that I was on parole, the perpetrators would have went free, and I'd have been the one in trouble. I'd be the one paying a thousand dollars to get out of Washtenaw County jail. That's why I kept walking."

One evening a few years prior to Percy's incident, I was walking to Farmer Jack grocery store with Carol, a good friend of mine. The last stretch was uphill, and Carol, who is an ardent walker and exerciser, was getting out of breath and slowing down. I was huffing and puffing even more, since I'd recently had minor surgery and did little or no exercise. Suddenly a cop car pulled up and two cops jumped out and ran over to Carol, who is white, to offer help. They wanted to know if I was bothering or hurting her. Carol pointed to me and shouted, "Help Rose, please." The officers looked at me in disbelief, returned to their car, and sped off.

"Rose, you tell me this all the time," she said afterward, "but this is the first time I've experienced it." She was appalled that I'd be treated like that. She assumed the community had moved beyond those types of attitudes.

Sure, it was dark and late and a white woman seemed to be struggling up the hill. Maybe they thought I was a crackhead about to pounce on her. Certainly they should stop and ask about our safety. But the assumption should not always be that a black person is about to commit a crime. We need to treat people with more equity and respect. Law enforcement needs to look at each situation carefully before drawing conclusions.

Just last year I received the kind of treatment I would hope for, and, frankly, it shocked me. I was turning into the parking lot for the Alano Club, a place where recovering alcoholics and drug addicts meet and socialize. There had been an accident on Maple Road and there were four police cars there. The street was clogged with cars and it looked like someone could get hurt if they weren't careful. So I slowed way down and took it real easy turning into the parking lot.

As I was getting out of the car, a white police officer came up and said, "Thanks, ma'am, for being so considerate and careful." I looked at him in disbelief, and one of two white guys with me said, "He ain't going to last long on the force."

The cop heard him. "Oh, there are a lot of officers around here who would be appreciative of you being so careful. There are cops in the street here and they could be run over."

"Sir," I said, "I've provided service in this city for more years than you are old. I've put what must be a million miles on my car providing service. Do you know how many times I've had an officer say to me what you just said?"

"How many?"

"One," I said. "Just now."

Then we thanked him profusely and wished him well. But I knew from experience just how quickly and effectively they would wear down an officer who was too polite and respectful of all citizens. My son Joe had been on the Ann Arbor police force and they drove him out.

Joe decided to become a police officer after an incident at the annual Rose Knows Retreat. Each year, I picked themes for the retreat to address concerns kids had been dealing with most of that year. In 1994 the subjects were understanding criminal intent and date rape, and the police came in and gave an hour-long presentation on the subjects.

Kids from all walks of life were there. The police talked about actions kids take that show criminal intent and how that affects the cops' behavior. Several kids brought the issue home by pointing out that just recently several white police had put some black kids in the dirt—making them lie there with their hands behind them for some minor infraction.

At one point in this discussion, a black fourteen-year-old from the back of the room raised his hand and asked, "Why aren't there more black police officers?"

"The black people who apply are not smart enough to pass the written test," the officer responded. The kids went into an uproar, and the other cop tried to put a more politically correct spin on the answer.

But the damage was done. Not long afterward, Joe, who'd been in the audience because he was a part-time counselor at the Peace Center, drew all his money out of the bank, quit his full-time job driving a bus for the Ann Arbor Public Schools, and paid his own tuition at the police academy at Lansing Community College. His reason: "Because that bastard had the nerve to stand there and say that and think nothing was wrong."

I was in tears the day they swore him in as an Ann Arbor police officer. And they weren't tears of joy.

"Joe, you can't make it," I told him. "I taught you to be a human being. The way you want to handle things and the way they want to do it are contradictory. Go somewhere else."

I'm sorry to say it, but my prediction was dead-on.

One afternoon near Briarwood Mall in Ann Arbor, Joe and his partner stopped a white kid for speeding in a brand-new, very expensive sports car. The kid came up with a lie, and Joe said his Field Training Officer (FTO), who was black, snatched this kid through the window, pushed him against the car, and started choking him, saying, "Motherfucker, you expect me to believe that shit?"

Joe pulled out his Mace at one point, and later the FTO asked him, "Were you going to Mace the motherfucker?"

"No," Joe said, "I was gonna Mace you. You were the one out of control. The kid was already scared, and the ticket would show we didn't believe him."

The officer, who was later promoted to sergeant, reported to his superior that he didn't think he could work with Joe, that he couldn't count on Joe to back him up in an emergency.

Another time Joe came home very depressed. He told me that four wealthy white kids had been caught stealing from Hudson's, an upscale department store now called Marshall Field's. Joe and his black partner arrived on the scene and the partner said he would call the parents. He told Joe to stay with the kids and interrogate them.

After about half an hour, a man came into the back room of Hudson's, where Joe was holding the kids. The man, obviously exasperated, turned to his daughter and said, "Beth, what else can we do? We've done everything, and now you're in Hudson's stealing." Joe said he almost cried hearing the man pleading with his daughter.

When Joe's partner arrived he asked the man what he was doing in the room.

"I need to know why my daughter is doing this," the man said.

"I told you to stay outside," the cop said, "so get outside."

"Sir," the man said, "I won't allow you to talk to me like that even if you are a police officer."

Then Joe's partner blew up.

"If you don't get out of here," he said, "I'll have you tied up in legal work for a year."

Joe said he was embarrassed. And so was I when I heard the story—but I wasn't surprised. I'm sorry to say that often the black cops, along with female cops, are worse than the white male officers. They've made their way into the system and they don't want to lose their place.

The straw that got Joe fired was actually an insignificant piece of paper. When Joe filled out his first written report of an incident, his commanding officer gave it back to him and told him it was not acceptable.

Since he'd never done this before, Joe got some research books on how to write police reports, stayed up all night to rewrite the report, and came to work a couple of hours early the next day to have one of the clerks type it neatly for him.

"Where did you get this?" the officer asked after Joe turned it in that afternoon.

Joe told him he had written it.

"Don't tell me you did this," the officer told him. "You couldn't have done this overnight. You cheated. Who did this for you? Was it your wife?"

The police department insisted, without proof, that Joe had cheated, and they gave him five days off with pay. After that suspension ended he was brought before the commanding officer and the police chief and asked for his resignation. At first he refused, telling them he had done absolutely nothing wrong. He reconsidered when they told him it would be easier for him to get another job if he resigned and was not fired. Besides, he'd been a top candidate for this job, he reasoned, so getting another one wouldn't be all that difficult. So before his one-year probationary period was up—after which he would have had union protection—he turned in his resignation.

What he hadn't anticipated was that the Ann Arbor Police Department would not only force him out, they would blackball him with comments made off the record—around the water cooler, in the locker room, and through various informal police networks.

Joe started applying and interviewing with other departments. Though his record with the Ann Arbor

Police Department read like a hymnal, he was unable to find a job despite more than thirty applications, countless interviews, and eighteen months of looking. The pain my son and our family had to endure was horrible. A living nightmare. And it nearly destroyed Joe and crippled our family economically. It is one thing to see the attack of an aggressor. It is still another to be cruelly victimized in the dark, never being able to identify the persons making the false and hurtful charges.

Finally the long search ended when he landed a job with a police department outside Ann Arbor. He has been with that department for five years and couldn't be happier.

"I don't have a clue what Ann Arbor was talking about," Joe's police chief told me at an open house. "We have had your son under a microscope for two years, looking for anything remotely resembling what Ann Arbor said would be a problem. I only wish we could give some of our other officers what your son has."

He said Joe's excellent communication skills were clear from the number of people who took the time to call or write the chief and tell him about their great experience with Joe. And that, he said, is rare, since most people call to complain, not to compliment an officer.

Joe is not the only family member who has had a bad experience with the local police department. My daughter-in-law, who graduated from the University of Michigan and worked for the police department as a community service agent for five years, decided to enter the police academy and become an officer.

During training, her sergeant told her that if she saw a black male driving a car that was over ten years old she should stop his car because chances are that he would either have tickets outstanding or be overdue on child support.

She objected to such profiling and said she wouldn't do it, to which she was told flatly, "If you're going to work here, you're going to do it."

Eight months into her field training, she was asked to resign. When she refused, they fired her. The same day she was let go there was a letter of commendation in her mailbox for how well she handled the situation when she was the first officer at a crowded scene where there had been a shooting death at a campus party.

But the Ann Arbor police aren't alone in their rudeness and arrogance. I went to the Washtenaw County Sheriff's Department not long ago. Apparently the office was being remodeled, but I didn't notice it. I went to the counter where people normally enter and stood there ten minutes with two other people, thinking that perhaps the deputy had just stepped away from the desk. Then I noticed the computer was unplugged, so I turned around and approached a desk across the room.

"Is that desk in operation?" I asked a female employee, pointing back to the entry desk we had been waiting at.

"No. Sit down," I was told.

I didn't sit down because I didn't like the way she ordered me, but I did move back from the desk and wait. After another fifteen minutes she finally called on me.

"I'd like to leave some money for a woman in jail," I said.

"That's not a quick question. You told me you had a quick question," she said.

I told her I had said no such thing. Realizing she wasn't going to intimidate me, she tossed the receipt at me, dismissing me as just another distraction.

Although it may seem a small thing, this kind of behavior from the first person the public has contact with at the Sheriff's Department sets the tone. It's not the kind of behavior that taxpayers, rich or poor, should have to tolerate. It is this constant abuse, constant sense of disdain you feel from the cops, that wears people down and makes them suspicious and resentful of them.

A client of mine named Lonnie B came home from work one night to find that the woman he had lived with for twenty-five years was leaving him for an eighteen-year-old. Lonnie B was taking his shirt off to wash up for dinner when she broke the news to him.

He started going crazy, breaking things in the house but not attacking her in any way. She called the police, who showed up in riot gear. Lonnie B had picked up a knife and was trying to stab himself. The police subdued him and put him in the patrol car.

Lonnie B's sister-in-law, Anna, and I came by the scene and found him without his shirt, shaking, in the police car. Anna tried to give the officer a blanket to put around her brother-in-law. The cops not only refused the help but also started berating her—calling this humble soul all kinds of nasty names. They charged Lonnie B with attempted murder of a police officer, even though all he had been trying to do was injure *himself* with the knife.

The next day, I went to the chief of police and pitched a bitch about how those officers had treated Anna. Two or three days later the two officers came to my office and apologized.

"Why apologize to me?" I asked them. "You didn't do anything to me. It's Anna you should be apologizing to."

But Anna, who had been embarrassed, insulted, and treated like dirt, never got so much as a letter or phone call apologizing for the treatment she received.

I had a run-in with a female officer of the Ann Arbor Police Department last fall that typifies this attitude of confrontation and disrespect. I'd had a busy Saturday running a yard sale for the Peace Neighborhood Center to raise money for our clients' personal needs. At the same time I was trying to help a client who had been evicted—giving him encouragement and attempting to find a place for him and his kids to stay for the weekend until the service agencies opened on Monday. I also had my grandson Blake with me for the day.

I was driving along with the client and my grandson, listening to the University of Michigan football game on the radio. Michigan blew the game at the end. My client was pissed. I was pissed. As we came down Maple Road we saw that two female cops had stopped a car. Three minutes later they were pulling us over.

Apparently as we passed by them my grandson had gotten out of his seat belt and was playing peekaboo with the cops out the rear window. They pulled me over for not having a seat belt on Blake. But it was soon clear that what really got under one of the officers' skin was that Blake was playing peekaboo. One of the female cops started getting hot about it and accused me of putting him up to it.

"Why else would he be lifting up and peeking down and doing all those things?" she asked.

"Because he's four years old and likes to play," I said. She didn't buy that simple and obvious answer, so she gave me a ticket instead of a warning.

I decided to take the ticket to court because it would cost me $75 I didn't have and affect my insurance coverage. Besides, I had put Blake in a seat belt when we left the Center and the fact that he was out of it temporarily was a simple oversight—not a conspiracy.

In court the officer told her story to the magistrate. When she was done, the magistrate asked for my side of things. I told him how my client and I were talking so furiously about Michigan blowing the game that I had failed to see that my grandson was out of his seat belt. (Happily, the magistrate was a big Michigan fan and shared our feelings about the defeat.) But, I told him, the little game of peekaboo was another matter.

"Your honor," I said, "I have lived in this city for thirty years, and one thing I don't do is teach children to deceive police officers. Especially my four-year-old grandson, who is a black male. If you think for one minute I'm going to teach him how to get killed by one of those arrogant SOBs, you've got another think coming. I'm not going to teach him something that could get him beat up."

The judge found me guilty of not having Blake in a seat belt but he dismissed the fine because I didn't know that Blake was unbelted. The female officer was so upset that the fine had been dismissed that I thought they might have to give her smelling salts. My being found guilty wasn't enough for her; she wanted her pound of flesh. I don't understand what it is with some police officers, male and female, that gets them to that point. What is it in their training or lives that causes them to get stuck on stupid?

FOURTEEN

To Hell and Back

$\mathcal{O}$N THE MIDST OF SAVING the world, I fell in love. I had been providing services in Ann Arbor for fifteen years—Mondays running into Sundays—when one day I suddenly realized that I was forty-four years old and hadn't kissed a man in more than ten years. A physical relationship with a man was one part of my life I had sadly neglected.

When I was younger I kept thinking "I'm only twenty-five" and then "I'm only thirty." A relationship with a man will happen in due course, I told myself. I was busy doing other things—serving other people, developing spiritually, getting high on life.

But now—at forty-four—I decided it was high time to get serious about a personal relationship. I talked with one of my girlfriends about this, and she told me, "No one wants to kiss you, Rose, because you're too particular, too straight. You've gotta make some compromises in order to be advertising for a man. If he's rugged and strong, you want to know if he would go camping with the kids. If he's got money, you want to know if he will give it to Mrs. Jones to keep her from being evicted. Honey, that's no way to lure a man."

I decided to call some married men I knew for help. I picked out three men who had character and one by one I asked them to lunch. I told them this was urgent — 911 on this one — and they figured I wanted to meet about a fundraiser or a program for the Peace Neighborhood Center.

When I met each of them at lunch I put forward my…well, my proposition.

"I want you to find a husband for me — someone with substance," I said. "And if you can't find a man of integrity, find me someone who will be a hell of a lot of fun."

They put out feelers, but despite their good efforts, no romantic prospects emerged.

Then one day, as I was headed for the post office on Main Street, a drunk stopped me.

"Ain't you Miss Rose?" he wanted to know. "Miss Rose, would you help me? I been back up in this alley praying for God to send me an angel, and I looked up and there you were."

"Why do you need an angel?" I asked.

"I want to get sober," he said. "I have been drinking like this for fourteen years and I'm thirty-two years old now. I've met a lot of people that you've sobered up, and I was wondering if you would help me."

I looked him over, thinking I recognized him.

"Aren't you the guy who had the fight at the shelter the other night?" I asked.

I'd taken a group of kids who were having a difficult time at home or in school to the shelter with me, as I often do. I'd bring them along to help out, and I'd say to the folks who run the shelter, "Save a bed for John (or Theresa or whoever was with me) because this is where they're headed if they don't change."

Earlier in the week when I was at the shelter I heard a ruckus when a fight broke out between two of the guys staying there. By the time I got to the top of the steps to see what was going on, someone stood alongside me and said, "I'm staff. I'll help you." I discovered soon enough that this savior was one of the guys who'd been doing the fighting.

And now here he was standing on the street begging me to take him in.

"You're the one who tried to trick me, aren't you?" I said. "You hit that guy and knocked him down."

But he continued to plead his case and I told him to come see me the next day at the Center and I'd see what I could do to help.

The following day, Marc showed up at the Center like he said he would. He stopped drinking immediately and went into our recovery program. After he'd been clean for about thirty days, he started asking me if I could help his brother who was drinking and doing drugs but wanted to quit. He said he wanted his brother to get on the wagon with this angel, just like he had.

"If you want to bring your brother," I said, "I don't have a problem with that."

Almost as quickly as the words were out of my mouth, I asked myself why the hell I'd said that. I barely had time to do what I needed to do and I tell Marc he can bring another person into recovery and start from day one. What was I thinking? There's enormous work that goes into saving someone from alcohol and drugs and then getting them integrated back into the mainstream. It's intense, to say the least.

I gave him the go-ahead at ten in the morning. By two in the afternoon I looked up and saw this man with hair like Wolfman Jack's and a beard you could walk on. He smelled like he wanted to be alone. Marc was beside him.

"This is my brother Christopher," Marc said. Then turning to his brother he added, "This is the angel I found. You can call her Rose."

Christopher looked up at me through his filth and the matted tangle of his beard with the most beautiful eyes I'd ever seen. They were brown, really nothing special physically, but there was an incredible depth in them. Despite his lowdown, dragged-out condition, those eyes glistened with some sort of higher power. I saw prayer in those eyes.

"Get him some clothes and something to eat," I told Marc. "He can stay with you at the motel you're staying at. Just be sure to take somebody else with you who's a little further into recovery so you can chat if Christopher feels like drinking." Then I went on about my business.

Several days passed and I heard through the staff that Christopher was making progress on his recovery. Then one night at about 6:30 I went through the Center, as I would most nights, to check on kids' homework, talk to staff and volunteers, give pep talks to people looking for jobs, and generally make sure everybody's needs were met for the evening.

This particular night I saw a man standing in the library off the main room. He was wearing black pants and a blue shirt. Talk about somebody fine. And remember, I'm already doing my look-for-a-man thing.

"Who *is* that?" I asked my friend and assistant, Nondi.

"I don't know," she said, "but all of our female clients have been coming through here, whispering and grinning." As I walked up to the library, I could only see his profile, but when he turned and looked at me, it was like Billy Dee looking at Diana Ross in *Lady Sings the Blues*.

Bitch, get ahold of yourself, I thought. Just the sight of this man was turning me on like you wouldn't believe.

Then Marc popped out of the library. "What do you think? I cleaned him up, cut his hair, and took him to the Red Shield store and got him some clothes."

This gorgeous man was Christopher, the scraggly drunk I'd seen before? Marc, I thought, you are a miracle worker.

After we chatted a bit, I realized this man was not only incredibly good looking, he was intelligent.

Afterward I turned to Nondi and said, "You've got to be his case worker. With how I'm feeling right now, it ain't going to work if I am. I don't want a conflict of interest."

As time went on, Christopher started coming to support groups. When he was there, I'd have someone else serve as facilitator because I was trying to distance myself. But no matter how hard I tried to separate myself from him, we kept being thrown together, finding ourselves at the same meetings or the same fundraisers.

One day Marc and Christopher came to me.

"Miss Rose," Marc said, "I've been clean all this time, and I didn't realize how much I liked women until I got clean. Before, all I wanted was another drink. Now, there's about seven of us living in an apartment, and we're all uptight. We can't have alcohol, can't have drugs, can't do this and can't do that. We have to do something to let off some steam."

Marc had already thought through his options and he presented them to me. One was to take the group to a whorehouse. Christopher just sat there smiling during his brother's discourse.

I ended up taking them to the Velvet Touch, an adult bookstore and peep show in town. I insisted on going along because there was no way they could go unsupervised since they were still in treatment. As I pulled up at the Velvet Touch, I thought about the people who ask why I didn't put Peace Neighborhood

Center's name on that van when we first got it. "There are some places this van goes," I said, "that I don't want the Center's name to follow."

I laid down only one condition for the visit: they couldn't go upstairs where the prostitutes were.

"We been here six months with no women," Marc protested.

"Why would you take advantage of someone who was put in the same position you were in?" I asked him. "Most of those women have the disease of addiction. They're selling their bodies because they haven't had anybody come along, pick them up, and take them on the road to recovery. How can you be six months into recovery and think of going down to ho' stroll? You can't feed yourself on the bodies of women taking drugs. You guys have to become human beings and talk to women who aren't being exploited. You need to go through all the bullshit other men go through."

I ran the whole thing on them. This was before AIDS, but I told them that by having sex with someone who may be shooting heroin, they ran the risk of introducing drugs into their own systems — something recovering addicts shouldn't do.

So I took them and dropped them off for a brief visit to the girly show. They all went in but Christopher, who suddenly seemed all the more attractive because he didn't go in. As we waited out the guys' R&R visit, Christopher and I eased back in the van and listened to my Luther Vandross tapes.

After four or five months, Christopher and I were spending a lot of time together, and our relationship was getting romantic. I was beginning to feel like the young schoolgirl that I'd never really had a chance to be. When we walked, we held hands. When we said goodnight, we kissed. We were building a solid friendship, and I wasn't worried about consummating the relationship right then. I was having too much fun enjoying the sexual attraction and having someone to share romantic feelings with.

And I was rediscovering a joyful, playful part of my personality. That's a part of you that's easy to lose when all your hours are consumed with the needs of drug addicts, the homeless, and abused children.

I was getting downright giddy. Christopher and I attended a recovery conference at the Holiday Inn. One evening I put on the swimsuit I had brought for the hotel pool. Knowing Christopher would be coming down the hallway for a workshop, I hid behind large curtains that covered the hallway windows. Balancing on a small ledge, no simple task for a full-figured woman, I stood behind the curtain for nearly a half-hour waiting for Christopher to pass by. When he was in sight I eased one bare leg out from behind the curtain and waggled it enticingly. Then covering my suit with the curtain to appear totally naked, I poked my head and chest out and did a little impromptu show as I struggled to maintain my balance on the narrow ledge. Christopher loved it and I managed to avoid tumbling from the ledge and breaking my neck.

Another time, I visited Christopher's apartment and was told by his brother that Chris was upstairs taking a bath. I headed for the bathroom, cracked the door, and found him sitting in the tub. With a big smile on my face, I headed straight for the tub and stepped right in—clothes, shoes, and all—and sat in the tub with him, much to his delight.

If I had found myself behaving like this any other time in my life, I swear I'd have asked to be institutionalized. Love does wonderful things to the mind.

Meanwhile, I was still trying to help the guys Christopher was living with. There was a place on Ellsworth Road where you could go and dance. I suggested we all go over there to let them shake off some of their anxieties. Five of us went and we danced and danced. On the way home they kept pleading, "Can we go back next Thursday? Can we go back next Thursday?" That night when I fell into bed I was so tired I could have screamed.

The next Thursday, the phone was ringing off the hook at Peace Neighborhood Center. When was I coming? They all had been to the thrift shops and the Red Shield secondhand store to get some "new" hookups. They were looking fine and raring to go.

I called my best friend, Mary, who is a nurse, and asked what time she was getting off work.

"I'll be off about seven. Why?"

"Because I caught hell last week trying to entertain all these guys by dancing with them until they warmed up enough to ask the other girls at this place to dance," I said. "Every record I was dancing with someone. It's not really my thing, but I was trying to keep the support system going for them. You know me — 'by any means necessary.' "

Mary, being the good friend she was, agreed to accompany me. This was the person who had worked at my restaurant, the Rosebowl, after her day job and had given me $500 of her hard-earned money to keep the restaurant afloat. Not only was she a beautiful person inside, men thought she was gorgeous.

We took a vacation together once, and one night after dinner we were walking outside the hotel and she said, "Rose, you're the only friend I have." I was shocked. I had known her for some fifteen years, and she seemed to me like someone everyone would want for a friend.

That night at the dance hall, Christopher was getting ready to dance, and normally he would have asked me. But Mary stepped up and said, "Can I dance with him?"

"Sure," I said, happy to have someone to fill in and give my tired feet a rest. Before the night was over Mary and I had danced with everyone several times over. When the place closed the guys in recovery left with big smiles on their faces, and Mary and I left with sore feet and a sense of accomplishment.

Seeing Christopher alone was getting to be a problem. Whenever I'd see him, his brother was usually hanging around. I got the brainy idea I'd introduce Marc to Mary, get him out of the picture, and accelerate my relationship with Christopher. I gave him Mary's phone number and suggested he give her a call since Mary was not seeing anyone and they might hit it off.

Marc made the call and set up a date with Mary, but the next day he told me she wasn't his type. At about the same time Christopher started calling or showing up less often. I asked him what was going on, and he said nothing had changed.

For about three or four weeks I didn't see Christopher at all, but we planned to get together again on a picnic at Hudson Mills Park out in the country along the Huron River. I love to drive into the woods at night, stop the car, lay back on the seats, and just lie out there and listen to the night sounds. It's one place I can escape all the worries and responsibilities of always being on call as a service provider. I'd taken Christopher with me on some of those jaunts and he liked it, too. We would drive back in the woods and sit in the van and just talk—not even hug or kiss or hold hands. It seemed so much easier to talk in the dark.

This time, however, we were going to go on a daytime picnic along the river, and I was excited.

"Kellyb, make me look real good," I told my daughter as she did my hair the day of the picnic. "I want to look special today."

Without warning Kellyb slammed the curlers she was putting in my hair down on the stove.

"The hell with them," she said, "you're my mother and I'm going to tell you. Remember when you came in here a few weeks ago and told me Christopher wasn't coming around as often and his manner had changed? That you thought there might be a mystery woman?"

"Yeah."

"Guess who the mystery woman is?" she said.

"Mary!" I nearly shouted without thinking. But even before the words were out of my mouth I had an image of Mary's car parked outside Christopher and Marc's apartment. Naively, I had assumed Mary might be visiting Christopher's brother. Just as quickly I recalled giving his brother Mary's phone number, and Christopher and Mary dancing together that night. The pieces started to fall in place and the picture they were making wasn't a pretty one.

"They said not to say anything to you because they loved you very much and they didn't want to hurt your feelings," Kellyb said.

"Kellyb, finish my hair."

When she was done I snatched the picnic basket off the kitchen table, got in the car—a big-ass Lincoln a friend had loaned me to take the kids at the Center on a trip—and went to pick Christopher up from his job. He was standing outside, and I suddenly got the urge to drive that big Lincoln up on the sidewalk and flatten him. But I pulled up alongside instead.

"Damn, you really turned up here fast," he said. "What's going on?"

As I sped toward the country he mentioned that he'd recently seen Ron, someone I dated ten years before.

"Don't come with that Ron shit," I told him. "I'm not such a sad case that you have to get me somebody first before you ask me to tell my story walking."

By that time, I was barrel-assing out along those country roads and had flown past the park. The next thing I knew I saw a sign that said "Hell, Michigan." I figured this was as good a place as any to start raising hell myself. I put on the brakes so fast his head jerked forward and bounced off the dash. Dust flew everywhere; it looked like a tornado.

"What is going on?" I said, repeating his words. "You ain't never seen this side of me. I knew there was a mystery woman and I found out this morning. Why didn't you and Mary come and tell me that y'all had a thing going on? You call yourself my friends?"

I really pitched a bitch up there in Hell before I finally calmed down.

"I'm really crazy going off like this," I said. "We never talked about this, but that's where my head took it. I went out of line. I shouldn't have gone there."

"You had every right to go there," Christopher said. "I'm sorry you did, but you had every right to."

And then he dropped the crushing blow. "I never promised you anything," he said. All those nights talking and dancing and kissing and hugging. All my schoolgirl shenanigans. All those wonderful glimpses into each other's hearts. Lying under the clear night sky—two souls brought together in the unfathomable reaches of space.

"I never promised you anything"? I could feel the bottom falling out right then and there. For all the abuse and grief I had suffered in my life, I'd never felt anything quite like this. I'd been abandoned by adults as a kid, but I'd never been double-crossed by a man. It was difficult. I loved Christopher on many levels — as an intelligent person, as a spiritual man with a good heart, and, I'd be lying if I didn't admit it, one fine-looking dude.

At the same time, my closest friend had betrayed me. For years Mary and I had talked at length about the unavailability of black men in our age group. They were either gay, in prison, on drugs, or had died in Vietnam. And she knew how I felt about Christopher, how I was trying to push up on him, have a romantic relationship.

Eight months after my short visit to Hell, I read in the paper that Christopher and Mary were engaged. Well, I thought, in the end they were a better fit for each other. She was moody, and so was he. They were both self-centered as hell. And Mary could get all giggly in a way I couldn't. Maybe he liked that.

Five years after they were married, Christopher came to the Peace Neighborhood Center to bring another person for help. I thought I had let it go, but the sight of him brought back a rush of feelings. He still looked as good as a government check. And show up here? That man sure had balls. But by the time he left I was relieved and released from the pain I'd been carrying for five years.

Christopher continued to stop by the Center from time to time, and he did some wonderful counseling with young kids on drugs. As a former addict and a strong, handsome man, kids listened when he spoke, and he spoke from the heart. Oh yes, he spoke from the heart.

I kept my distance from him, and I'd be hard on him when he was in my presence. I kept a wall up between us and he knew not to cross it.

Then one day many years after we'd parted ways, I was in the kitchen at the Center leaning over a pot of bean soup, cooking lunch for the kids. But lunch was the last thing on my mind. My baby Kellyb, who'd grown up to be a smart, capable young woman, had suddenly become addicted to drugs. And right now that bright light of my life was lying in bed at home, broken and battered by a pusher she'd tried to steal drugs from.

I was helpless. The sheer terror that only a mother with a child on drugs can know had gripped my heart for a month.

I'd been up most of the night praying and worrying. "Lord," I said, "I've helped many of your children kick the curse of drugs. *Please* send me someone who can help with my baby." I knew I couldn't do it for Kellyb because obviously I was one of the sources of the problem.

Staring into that pot of soup—the hot steam mixed with my own tears—I was still praying. Suddenly beside me was Christopher.

"What the hell are you doing here?" I asked.

"I don't know," he said. "But I got up this morning and my feet wouldn't take me anyplace but here. Why you crying?"

I couldn't hide this pain. I told him about Kellyb and how no one could reach out to her and bring her back from this horrible addiction.

Without hesitation, Christopher asked where she was. I told him where he'd find her and he left. The next thing I heard was that afternoon when I got a call from the recovery center. They wanted to let me know my daughter was there and would be going through treatment. She'd been brought there by a man named Christopher.

Kellyb, after eighteen long months in recovery, emerged not only clean, but also more whole and wonderful than ever. We just recently celebrated her eighth year off drugs.

Folks who run into Christopher these days say he tells everybody I'm his spiritual mother. Isn't that something? Always a mother or a sister. Never a bride.

ATTACK

*I LIKE TO WALK THREE OR FOUR MILES A DAY, but I don't
do it in the daytime because people run up to me and stop me
and give me more work to do.*

*One night in the spring of 1999, I was walking down
Washtenaw Avenue on the outskirts of Ypsilanti. It was about
11:30 at night, and I had just visited a couple there because the
husband was having a problem with his job.*

*I noticed a carload of white kids drive by in an old Buick.
They turned into the Ypsi-Arbor Lanes bowling alley and
stopped. As I got close, they pulled out of the parking lot driveway and started yelling obscenities at me as they drove by. They
went about a quarter of a mile, turned around, came back,
stopped the car, and got out. I think there were four of them in
the car but I only saw three get out.*

*Then they began pelting me with something—I couldn't
tell what. All I knew is that it hurt and I was as scared as I've
ever been. I fell to the ground and covered my face so they
wouldn't hurt my head or blind me. I had just had open-heart
surgery two months earlier, and I was afraid that they would
cause major damage. I was praying they wouldn't kill me.*

*Whatever it was they were hitting me with turned wet
when it smashed into me and it smelled something awful. The
stink was so wretched I threw up.*

*The whole incident didn't last more than a minute, but it
seemed like three days. When I finally heard them drive off, I*

looked up from under my arms, but they were too far away to identify. Those bastards actually had the nerve to stop at the traffic light. Then a man and a woman came out of a grocery store, saw me on the ground, and came over to help me.

When I got home I washed my hands over and over again. Then I took a bath, and then another. I could still smell the stench. I had enormous bruises, and three weeks later, it still hurt when I turned a certain way. But the fact that I couldn't defend myself hurt more than the physical pain. I felt defenseless and alone.

This happened about the time a black man had been dragged to his death in Texas.

FIFTEEN

Thorns for a Rose

$\mathcal{F}$OR ABOUT TWO MONTHS DURING the spring of 1992 I had been working sixteen or seventeen hours a day, Monday through Sunday, and I was dead tired.

One project that had taken up a lot of my time was getting an old man out of Michigan's Jackson State Prison. He had no business being there in the first place. The judge sentenced him to prison because he had no place else to put him. Basically, he'd been sentenced to prison for being homeless.

Paddy Malone would wander the streets, occasionally getting into mischief. He suffered from unexplainable seizures and had been in and out of mental hospitals. But this seventy-year-old man was no candidate for prison, and I was so outraged by his sentence of one to three years in the state penitentiary that I worked my butt off to get him out.

It took well over a year and the help of a couple of my affluent friends, but on the morning of June 20, I jumped into my twenty-year-old car and drove the thirty-five miles to Jackson Prison to pick him up.

When he got in the car, he told me he was hungry.

"We don't have any money right now," I told him, "but when we get back to Ann Arbor, I'll find us something to eat. You'll have to hold on that long, okay?"

"I am so glad to see you, Ms. Martin," he said in an Irish brogue that belied the fact he'd been in this country forty-five years. He thanked me for sticking with him, for making sure he had cigarettes, and for visiting him.

As we walked into the Peace Neighborhood Center to see if we could scare up some food for my friend, I was elated that all the work had paid off. I was greeted as I entered by our board vice president, John Cedric Simpson, then a lawyer and now a judge in Washtenaw County. His family had helped establish the Peace Neighborhood Center and he had virtually grown up there.

"There's some trouble," Simpson said.

"Tell me about it later," I said. "I got a hungry guy to feed."

"No, I have to tell you now," he insisted. There were tears in his eyes.

"Rose," he said, "Eric Stalhandske and Frank Moore have it in their minds that you are mismanaging funds, and they are striking up support for your dismissal. This is going to be a horror story." Eric had until recently been the president of the Center's board

ONE ROSE BLOOMING

of directors. He also was a bean counter for the Veterans Administration where he was instrumental in toppling some top official for misuse of funds. Frank Moore had been treasurer for the Center's board of directors. Both resigned from the board in April 1992.

If I had been going to bed every night at nine or ten o'clock I might have taken this a little better. But I was so worn out I could hardly respond.

"Do I need a lawyer?" was all I could say.

"Yes, you need a lawyer."

He pulled out an article from the *Ann Arbor News* that had been in the paper that day, June 20, 1992. The headline screamed, "City plans to audit Peace Center," and where the story broke over to a second page, "HUD may join audit."

I slumped down in the chair as he read it to me. The story opened, "After receiving complaints of financial mismanagement at Ann Arbor's Peace Neighborhood Center, city officials plan to audit the non-profit agency's books...Two PNC board members resigned in April after other board members refused to approve financial management changes that the two had recommended...The focus will be on the spending and record-keeping of PNC Director Rose Martin, a popular leader for the last 17 years."

"Do you think I'm guilty?" I asked John.

"Absolutely not," he said, "but I do know that your methods of getting things done are unconventional and that you leave yourself open for anybody to take a shot at you. At this point, I'm not so sure that the outcome will be good for you, not to mention how much the Center is going to suffer because of this being on the front page of the paper. What do you suppose happened to cause this?" John asked.

Cause it? Hell, there was nothing to cause it. All my career I've taken chances because to get things done for people you have to take chances. I could play it safe and everyone in officialdom would love me. But it wouldn't get the job done.

I did things in an unorthodox way simply because I knew it worked. I might put someone up in a nice motel for $79 a night when I could have put them in a bare-bones joint for $34. But I'd do it to get their attention. And once I had their attention, I could begin connecting with them to help them off drugs or to learn how to be a better parent. When you're trying to reach someone, you need to gain their trust. If that meant cooking them steaks at my home rather than sending them to a soup kitchen, then so be it.

I didn't have time to fool around with all the niceties of bureaucracy. But I never imagined my methods would ever put at risk all that I did and all I that hoped to do. I could feel the bottom dropping out and it shook me to my core.

I immediately thought back to a conversation I had with Rich Ballard some months earlier. Rich tried to warn me. He had been president of the board of directors at the Center for eight or nine years and would be leaving the board. Before he stepped down as president in nine months, he said, I should give serious thought to who would succeed him.

"This is important," he said, "because you do

things in such an unorthodox way. You're highly successful, but I can see you having a problem with a board president if you don't select someone who is open, someone who can accept and appreciate the way you get results."

He was right, but at that time I had a dozen other things that needed immediate attention. Before long, however, the nine months had elapsed and Eric Stalhandske became president of the board in December of 1991. He'd been on the board three years, hadn't ruffled any feathers, and lived next door to the South Maple public housing site. I never imagined there would be a problem.

The first thing Eric tried to do after becoming president was change our bank. I fought him tooth and nail because our bank gives us a lot of chairs and tables, hires our teens, cashes checks for our clients who don't have IDs, and provides a lot of other services to our program.

Then he tried to change our auditing company. I fought him again because the auditing company we were using had done so many good things outside of keeping our books. Everything Eric came up with got shot down. He even came up with an asinine plan to ensure that no one would get more than $50 from Peace Neighborhood Center in any thirty-day period.

In those days, money came into the Center in nickels and dimes, so I was spending it as it came in. Eric would see the revenues at the end of the year—$200,000 to $300,000—and wanted some say-so in how it was spent.

Prior to Eric's resignation, he had come to my office and asked me why it was that he and I couldn't get along. Anytime he came up with something, he said, I shot it down, and that made it difficult for him to act as board president. I told him, "You know, Eric, it sounds like a personal problem to me. Maybe you should go home and talk to your wife about it."

He bolted up in his chair and said, "I'm your worst nightmare," and walked out. As he left, I turned to my assistant director and said, "Boy, that was a strong threat. But how can he hurt me? I don't have a damn thing." Then I went back to dealing with the children.

On Friday of that week, I had to take a client to a treatment center in Pontiac at eight in the morning. I didn't get back to the Center until eleven. When I walked in, a member of the staff called me aside and said Eric and Frank Moore had been in earlier that morning taking pictures of all the transactions I had made. They had asked for the MasterCard and telephone bills.

Prior to their resignations, Eric and Frank held secret meetings with the other white board members. I learned of this when one white board member, Mary Watkins, was told by the board secretary that an emergency meeting was planned among just the white board members. On the agenda was the issue of my supposedly mismanaging funds. When Mary asked the board secretary why there would be no black board members present, she said it was because the white board members thought that black board members wouldn't look at the problem objectively. They thought they would be too gung-ho for Rose.

God bless Mary Watkins. Today I give her credit for saving Peace Neighborhood Center because she had the character and spiritual maturity to question that meeting and then telephone Peace's vice president, who also had not been invited. Otherwise, I might have been kicked out before I knew what was happening.

After John broke the news to me and showed me the *Ann Arbor News* story, I took the still-hungry Paddy Malone to a friend of mine's house, where he would be taken care of, and then opened the phone book I always carry in my car.

As I turned to the section on attorneys, I remembered Tom O'Brien, an attorney in town who had helped me out so many times pro bono with my clients. Tom was not only a hell of a good attorney; he had a heart as big as Washtenaw County. So I put down the phone book and started driving toward his office. About halfway there, it dawned on me that I had no money to hire a lawyer, and I knew Tom was expensive. But I decided I should talk with him anyway and showed up without an appointment.

After about twenty-five minutes, he took me into his office. I told him what had just happened and that John had said I needed a lawyer.

"There's only one thing here we need to talk about," I said, "and that's money. I don't have any, not a dime. But if I had any money, what would it cost to have you represent me?"

"You would need a retainer of five thousand dollars," he said. "If federal charges are brought against you, legal fees for the full trial could go as high as fifty thousand dollars, maybe more."

Tears were running down my cheeks.

"But," Tom said, "I've seen how you've worked with people. You're one of my local heroes, and there's no way you could do what you do and have money. If you promise me one thing, I will represent you pro bono all the way to the United States Supreme Court."

"What's that?" I said.

"I don't want you giving out statements and talking to people about this particular situation, creating more work for me and this firm when we're doing this for you pro bono. If you start giving out statements, there's going to be a problem. If anybody asks you anything as it relates to this situation, direct them to me."

Later that day the *Ann Arbor News* called me at work for comment and I directed them to Tom O'Brien, as he had requested. Tom answered their questions more eloquently than I ever could have, and it was in the paper that night that he was representing me.

At the next board meeting, which took place a week or two later, I listened in shock as one of the folks who were against me said, "We told you she was stealing money. Tom O'Brien is representing her. If she isn't taking money, how can she afford to have him represent her?" I couldn't speak up about the arrangement with Tom because of my vow of silence, so I let the comment pass. In fact, this is the first time I've told my side of the story publicly.

It wasn't long before the city of Ann Arbor was joined by the U.S. Department of Housing and Urban Development, United Way, and other foundations and private contributors in looking at our funding and expenditures. Vincent Buccirosso, director of United Way at the time, had heard from Eric, Frank, and a disgruntled employee named Kevin Kelly; they had told him there was a glaring problem related to the expenditure of money at the Center. Instead of Vince contacting my board and bringing them together to resolve the matter, he called the Community Development Block Grant agency, through which we got our city funding, and other people to alert them that my former board president and treasurer were bringing allegations against me.

John Simpson went to Vince and asked him why he would go to the city and newspaper before speaking to the Peace Neighborhood Center board. I think Vince felt bad about that, but by this time the ball was rolling, and things were getting ugly.

Vince called us and told us he had an obligation to investigate the charges, and until the investigation was done, he would have to hold up our monthly check from United Way. Then he gave us an order we shouldn't have been able to fill. We had written 2,455 checks and he had a machine that would randomly pick three hundred of them by number. He wanted to see the backup receipts for those randomly picked checks, and he gave us thirty days to come up with them. This was at 4:30 on a Friday afternoon.

When I got back to Peace Neighborhood Center, Marcia, a woman who had worked with us years before, was there to help, along with several other past staff members, directors, and former clients. We stayed there from Friday night through Sunday night. By 8:30 on Monday morning, we were at United Way with the backups for those three hundred checks.

Although we were by no means a bureaucracy with detailed dossiers on every transaction, we were able to present a clear picture of where the payments went—clients' names, services provided, and that sort of thing. If we wrote a check for $200 to Kroger for groceries, we had a receipt from Kroger and a statement from the client as to what they had received.

Vince and his staff were amazed that we were able to back up our expenditures so well after what they had been told by our accusers. The United Way accounting people looked over our documentation and saw that the expenditures were legitimate, and United Way dropped its sanctions against the Center after some four days and suggested minor bookkeeping controls. On June 28, 1992, the *Ann Arbor News* reported that Vince Buccirosso said: "We're satisfied that basically the financial integrity of the group is intact, otherwise their funding would have ceased."

The accounting firm of Deloitte & Touche, which had done the Center's books for some ten years, said they had "never found any evidence of significant problems."

Despite the evidence that Peace Neighborhood Center and I were not up to any shenanigans, it seemed as though everyone who ever gave us a dime more than breakfast money was sending auditors. On July 9 it was announced that the city put on hold a $60,000 grant we had been given for our summer youth camp. The city released $15,000 of the grant later in the month, only after several supporters of ours, including former mayor Bob Harris and attorney Ron Gregg, said they would post personal assets as collateral for the grant in case the city found any improprieties and demanded the $15,000 be returned.

When I saw a copy of the agreement these supporters had made—and didn't even tell me about—Gargantua couldn't have held me back. It was like getting a new breath of life. In about a week, Peace Neighborhood Center programs were operating to capacity. We were getting staggered pay, and we did a lot of juggling, but it worked out. The money saved the summer camp program, which each year is attended by some one hundred children from low-income households.

At the beginning of September 1992, HUD announced that federal investigators would be looking at all our files for the past four years. On September 2, the *Ann Arbor News* reported:

> As the federal Department of Housing and Urban Development seeks Peace documents, John Hambrick, a HUD assistant inspector general in Chicago, said Peace is one of only a dozen organizations throughout a six-state Great Lakes

region to be probed this year for allegedly mis-spending government grants.

"We're pretty picky about who we investigate," Hambrick said, adding that about 80 percent of such investigations result in penalties ranging from criminal charges to a ban on future federal funding.

"I think we'll fall in that 20 percent (of investigations that find no wrongdoing)," said J. Cedric Simpson, Peace's acting board president.

The investigators were calling into question deferred overtime payments to a long-time employee who had worked at our summer camp; spending on bus trips for the children at the Center; and support for people staying off drugs.

One of the investigations reported that Rose Martin had checks totaling $60,000 made out to her personally. It sounded like I had used that money for myself, but the reason I received the checks was that if we were going to the Toledo Zoo or Cedar Point amusement park or the Jackson Space Center with a busload of eighty kids, I had to pay for them in cash. So I would get our accountant or office manager to write a check to me, and then I would cash it and use the money to do what I was going to do regarding Peace's programs and bring back receipts. Plus, when we provided money to support clients, it often had to be in cash because many of them did not have bank accounts.

The nightmare continued, and it began to wear us down and threaten our existence. In early 1993, HUD ordered the Ann Arbor Community Development

Director to "under no circumstances" make any additional community development grant payments to the Center. At that time we had received only $30,000 of a $60,000 appropriation from the city.

Our fundraising was suffering and we were virtually powerless to defend ourselves until the audit was over, and when that would be was anyone's guess. I maintained my silence on the matter, as I had promised.

One investigator—I think he was from HUD— said to some other people that my life was a joke. I didn't smoke. I didn't drink. I didn't do drugs. And I didn't have any bad habits that cost money. I had no hidden area of my life that was out of control and required money. Except food. All they had to do was look in my refrigerator and see that I eat like a Brahma bull. But even I couldn't eat $60,000 worth of food in a year.

When the inspector looked in my safe-deposit box, without permission, he was really spooked. I had letters my kids had sent me from summer camp, a picture and a letter from a guy whom I loved twenty-five years ago, the eyeglasses from when my son was two years old, and the report cards of my children. I saved the report cards so that when my kids start getting on my grandchildren about their report cards, I could hop down to the bank, pull out their parents' cards, and say, "What grade are you in? Here's your daddy's report card from that year. Is his any better?"

While all of this was dragging on, some of my most ardent supporters were getting a little too worked up. I had a client who had served three long stints in the penitentiary come to my office one day with a .38 pistol ready to do Eric Stalhandske in.

"He's a dead man," he said. "I don't want you to worry, Ms. Martin. I will take care of you."

"If you do that, I will leave this job today," I told him. "I will not have blood on my hands. Haven't I taught you anything regarding peaceful solutions to problems? Put the word out on the street: If any of you harm a hair on this man's head—or his wife or his children—I'm out of here. And get out of here with that gun before it goes off accidentally and somebody gets hurt."

I had at least three criminals come to me with plans they were going to carry out to save me. I squelched all of them. I provided a big picnic one afternoon and gave a speech in which I told them, "Protect him. I want his house watched day and night." The first three weeks after the story broke in the papers, his house was watched twenty-four hours a day by people who made sure some crazy person didn't do something rash, which was easy since his house was adjacent to the public housing site and people from the project could sit near his driveway all night.

Protecting Eric—and Frank and Kevin, for that matter—was one of the most difficult things I've had to do in my life because of the devastating hurt they had caused me, but I was adamant that no one would harm them in any way. I would not have been able to live with that.

The trauma continued to mount. People who had given money in the past were hesitant and our revenues started to fall. I felt so demoralized during this whole time that I would sit down at Peace Neighborhood Center and do nothing for days.

But there were also plenty of folks who stood tall and wouldn't let us fail. It was that love and support that kept me from going crazy or having a nervous breakdown. Every day seemed to bring a new measure of love from some group or individual in this town, including people I least expected to hear from and people whom I had not heard from in ten or fifteen years.

Despite the support, it looked like we would have to close the door at the Center for good. As my assistant and I were leaving one day, not knowing how long we could keep it all together, Jack and Jean DiGiuseppi pulled into the parking lot and walked over.

"We heard what they said about you," Jean said. "We know you don't have money, so Jack and I brought you some."

"I don't think it's smart to give that to a thief," I said. She responded that she didn't think it was smart not to give it to me, that it was to show how much they trusted me and how important it was to keep the doors open.

The next day a woman, looking as old as the queen mother but dressed like a ragamuffin, came to the Center. She walked up to me and handed me a grocery bag. I looked in and saw so many $20, $50, and $100 bills that I said to myself, It's a plant. Get out of town, bitch. They're coming after you. They're setting you up.

"No, ma'am, I'm not touching that money," I said to her.

She said it was her money to give.

"My neighbors have had personal experience with you helping their children," she said. "My daughter is a teacher in the Ann Arbor Public Schools and when she comes to dinner, she often talks about what you've done to help children. Dammit, if you're stealing, when do you take the time off to spend the money? Every time I come by here, you're here."

"Thank you, ma'am," I said, "but you have to give me a check. I'm in enough shit." So one of our volunteers went to the bank with her and got a cashier's check.

Somehow that gift was a watershed. From that day on people started coming to help.

If there are angels walking around today on planet earth, Orval Willimann, the past minister of Bethlehem United Church of Christ, is one of them. We reached a point where most of our employees were about to have their lights turned off or be evicted because they had been working without pay for some time.

Orval came over one day and said, "It just dawned on me this morning: I know you don't have any money coming in, and I was wondering how you guys were making it personally." Everybody there just broke down and started crying, but Orval was as nonchalant and matter-of-fact as he could be. He bought us food, took care of things that we needed to have done for us personally. He made no bones about it—didn't call us out like beggars on the street. He just came and helped.

Then on December 8, 1994, some two and one-half years after the news broke, we received a letter from the assistant U.S. attorney. "This is to inform you that this office has determined that criminal prosecution in the above-captioned matter is not warranted." They noted that they disagreed with the billing of certain expenses to federal block grants, for which the city would have to reimburse them, but the Center and I were cleared of all the nasty charges that had been leveled against us. Maybe we weren't the best bookkeepers in the world, but we had a lot of love going for us.

The long investigation had cost us dearly, to say nothing of what it cost the taxpayers. Private and city donations to the Center had plunged about $100,000 over the previous two years. Several programs, including after-school activities for youths, were severely cut. Other programs, like the annual Thanksgiving meal and the weekly family spaghetti dinner, had been eliminated altogether.

But we were back. And I was jumping for joy to know that what I believe in—sharing and caring for people—really does work. They say that what you give is what you get back. But I think that what came back to me and this community was greater than anything I'd been able to give over the years.

SIXTEEN

Keeping Good Company

*E*VERYONE NEEDS MENTORS. Especially children. That's why I think it's so important that adults take an active role in the lives of kids. We need to provide them with sources of inspiration, examples of how to cope with the rough times they will inevitably have to face.

I've been fortunate to have some exceptional people in my life who have provided inspiration and guidance. These are people who I think about when I get tired, overworked, or frustrated. My heroes are individuals who encouraged others to do the best they could. Folks who respected and valued all people, who wouldn't be stopped by adversity. I think about them and I am renewed in spirit, and I can go on.

Daisy Gray

Miss Daisy Gray was my first mentor. I met her when I was about five or six years old. She lived next door and was about thirty at the time. She lived with her husband, daughter, mother, and her deceased sister's two children.

Miss Daisy always looked neat and clean every day she went to work at a cigar factory. At home she had to deal with a husband who drank and raised hell most of the time. He would get obnoxious and loud, but she would always be very calm and loving and quiet him down. She had a way of keeping things in their place and working to resolve problems.

But the part of Miss Daisy that impressed me the most was that she always had a compliment for you. She would come to her door and call out for a kid to run to the store for her. That's the way they would do in those days in the inner city; kids would play in front of the houses and someone might come to the door and offer them two cents or a nickel to run an errand. When I ran an errand for Miss Daisy, she would always say, "You are so smart. You are really going to be something some day. You always remember everything I wanted and bring me back the correct amounts and brands. Although you're poor, you're going to rise above this and be a great adult."

Often I'd meet her just in passing and she'd wink and say, "You're special." Do you know how much that little greeting meant to a kid who was kicked in the teeth and teased mercilessly in school?

When I was a kid they would hold what they called "Tom Thumb weddings" in black churches. The congregation would sell tickets to the community as a fundraiser for the church. The preacher would usually be about nine years old, the bride and groom about five or six, and the flower girls two or three. The groom would have on a tuxedo and the bride would be in a wedding dress made by the women of the church. Being the bride was a much-sought-after role of every girl in the neighborhood.

One year Miss Daisy not only chose me, she fussed over me. I had nappy hair, and she pressed it with a hot comb and curled it and talked about how pretty I was. My hair did look nice, and the kids stopped teasing me that week. I told Miss Daisy I wished I could have stayed like that forever.

After that, for as long as we lived on Liberty Street, Miss Daisy would take me into her home every two weeks to do my hair. I knew she had work to do. I knew she was tired. I knew she had to deal with her asshole husband, as well as her mother and her deceased sister's two kids. But every other Sunday afternoon she would call me into her home, wash my hair, hot press it, and wrap it up in a stocking cap so it would look good in the morning.

I hope I can be to children what Miss Daisy was to me.

Olive Pontier

When I was a child, adults were not in the habit of giving explanations for their actions to kids. If you asked certain questions of adults, you were likely to get slapped down or admonished. Kids were taught to stay in their place, to be seen and not heard.

Mrs. Olive Pontier was different. She was at least forty years my senior, and I met her when I went to the Florence Crittenden home for unwed mothers. Although she was not one to bend the rules at the home, I could talk with her about things I was thinking and it wouldn't upset her. Other adults would get upset when I asked where God came from, and why there was prejudice, and what color God was, and why some people had so much and other people didn't have a thing.

In that winter of 1961 there was a lot of conflict between blacks and whites, rich and poor. Mrs. Pontier transcended all that. You could tell it by the way she treated you, the way she behaved. I think she was the first true Christian white person that I had met.

One of the answers she gave to my questions that I like best was when she explained to me why innocent children get polio or are deformed or die from heart problems. She told me it didn't mean that God was cruel or that He wasn't all-merciful. She said God gives us tests. No soul is tested beyond its ability to perform, but some souls pray for an elevation to a spiritual level so high they have to withstand such a test to get there. They have prayed for things that made it necessary to get through those tests to be ultimately happy at a higher spiritual level once they leave their mortal frames.

Rich Ballard

Some people are so real and genuine and loving, they are like a breath of fresh air. Rich Ballard is one of those people. He's not afraid to stick his neck out, not afraid to take chances to help others.

I first met Rich Ballard more than twenty-five years ago when he was a special reading teacher at Huron High School. And I've been singing his praises ever since. I never thought I would truly love a white man, though I never felt like I was racist or anything like that. But the love I have for Rich is the same kind of love I have for my brothers and my kids.

It didn't come easily because I'm not easy. I observe people, and you have to be consistent to impress me. I don't watch what comes out of your mouth. I watch your actions. It comes from growing up on the streets and constantly being at the mercy of strangers. You can't afford to get fooled, like plenty of people do, by someone who just talks a good game or by those who want to impress you with how much material wealth they have. I watch what you do. And when I watch what Rich Ballard does, I am impressed with what a tremendous human being he is.

What I admire about Rich is that he will go the whole mile and ask nothing in return. As a teacher he has taught untold numbers of kids to read, doing whatever was necessary to make it happen for those children. He was one of those who spearheaded the New School project in Ann Arbor. The New School was established as a place for kids who had problems excelling in the traditional school system. This experimental school, begun in 1996, never had enough money to operate and went belly-up after less than four years in operation. Still, it made a measurable difference in the lives of many children.

Right now I can see the kids' faces—black and white—that won't get the opportunity they would have had if the New School were still in existence. There's one kid I know who could be the next director of the Peace Neighborhood Center, but I bet she won't reach that potential because she is disenchanted with the traditional school she's in. Instead of being abandoned and dismantled, the New School should have been rewarded for the creativity that teachers like Rich Ballard used in teaching kids to read.

I've also known Rich in other circumstances. I remember a man who came into the Peace Neighborhood Center high as hell on heroin and carrying a baby in his arms. Rich was on the Center's board of directors at the time and he was at the Center on business. He dropped everything he had to do that day and got on the phone and helped me raise money to get this man into a treatment center. Then he put up his own money to help take care of the man's baby and feed his family. As always, Rich didn't look for anything in return. He didn't say, "I need my lawn mowed, let's get this man to do it," or "Let's get him to help me build my garage." He did it and we moved on to the next person who needed our services.

Rich is like a candle that burns and burns and burns, giving off light right down to the end. There have been times when I've had enough and I was ready to quit on a particular project, but Rich was always there with something to say that made me understand that quitting wasn't an option.

Erma Hayden

If you told me you'd been down to Lake Michigan and saw someone out walking on water, I wouldn't be surprised to learn it was Erma Hayden. In street language, she was the doo-doo. Her husband, Robert, was a renowned poet who read for both the Senate and the president of the United States. She was an accomplished pianist herself. But most important, Erma was one great human being.

When I was in my twenties, a bunch of us young girls would go over to Erma's house on Wednesday or Thursday evenings and talk about things that were bothering us. She was there for all of us. Most of all, Erma taught me that the material world moves faster than the spiritual world. If you're thinking of spiritual solutions to problems, you're going to move slower because you have to take into consideration the feelings of others before you make your decisions.

When I met Erma, I was doing a lot of living in the material world and making quick, selfish decisions. Erma taught me to consider other people's feelings in every decision I made. If we were in a restaurant and she saw an old person approaching, she'd insist we move to a table farther back so the older person could have the closer table. She would never try to beat someone to a parking space. In fact, there were times when I would say to her, "Erma, why are we parking all the way back here?" And she would say, "Did you see the lady coming in behind us? Did you see the four children she had with her? She's going to have to wrestle those four kids to the door. We can walk."

Erma was always celebrating people's birthdays by bringing them a homemade cake or pie or taking them to a special place for lunch because they had done something wonderful. If you had four or five kids and hadn't killed any of them that week, she would come to your house, pay for a baby-sitter, and take you to a nice restaurant for lunch. Then she'd tell you what a great mother you were. It didn't matter what color you were or what your religious background was.

During one of the gatherings at Erma's living room, five of us girls were gossiping about the town prostitute. Now, Erma did not like gossip. You could not catch her gossiping, and if she found you gossiping she would just give you a soft smile that would make your catty words drop like a thousand-pound weight. As we were carrying on about this girl, calling her a whore and a horrible person and all, Erma had taken about all she could.

"Shame on you, girls," she said, "talking about this young woman like this. You could learn something from her."

Is Erma suggesting we become whores, we thought?

"Rather than condemn this woman," she said, "think of her capacity for love. I understand that what she's doing is not socially acceptable, but she has to have something inside her that is so giving in order for her to be a pleaser like she is."

Erma taught us to look beyond the social ills and the things we didn't like about a person, to look deep inside to find the good.

I couldn't help but flash back to when I was a kid in Camden. Some of the best people to kids in the neighborhood were the women in the whorehouse that Miss Honey ran. They were always clean. They were always fair. They wouldn't send you to the store and not give you money. If you had something special going on in school, they might bring you a nice cardigan sweater or something special to wear. And if you fell and skinned your knee, they would always wash it and put a bandage on it.

They were good people who never touched us inappropriately, never cussed around us, and never took advantage of us in any way. But I can tell you the names of some deacons who sat on the front benches in the churches who did—I can give you a long list of those folks. But the people who lived in that whorehouse on the corner were always talked about like the dregs of the earth. To me, they were the best.

When I was sixteen, it was one of those prostitutes who took me to the hospital when she found me beaten up and bleeding on the street. She even made provisions for me to stay in a boarding house temporarily after I got out of the hospital.

So when Erma made us think about this girl's capacity for love and understanding, it made sense to me. Who but Erma Hayden would even think of that? She always knew what was right.

Helen McCluskey

Helen was cut from the same cloth as Erma. She and her husband, Howard, lived for about fifty years in a house on Liberty Street next to Zion Lutheran Church. One day I was flying past their house on my way to city hall and saw one of the town's worst characters raking leaves and cleaning up the yard. This man was a dope fiend and someone you wouldn't want around your home under any circumstances.

I put the brakes on, turned around, and drove back to her house, scared to death. When Helen came to the door she was just as delighted and giddy as she could be.

"Look how well he did my blinds," she said.

"Was he *in* this house?"

"Yes," she said. "He knocked on my door and was looking for work. Howard and I are up in years now, so I put him to work."

"Helen, that might have been okay in 1940, but it's not okay in 1985," I told her. "You can't do that. There's too much crack cocaine around, too much dope."

She remained steadfast. "He told me he'd give me an honest day's work for an honest day's pay."

I caught up with him one day when he was away from Helen and told him, "Listen, nothing in the drugstore will kill your ass quicker than me and those who love Helen if you ever do anything to harm a hair on that woman's head or take anything out of her house."

"You can forget me ever taking anything from her," he said. "It hasn't even entered my mind. After the love that woman showed me when I knocked on her door? Unh-unh. You only see love, I think, once in your life. I see love in that woman."

Here was a guy who would steal the fire out of hell and he ended up working for her until the day she died. He'd go to her house one or two days a week and do chores for her. This is a man who stole his hardworking mother's life savings to buy drugs, but he never stole one thing from Helen.

If you had a thousand glaring bad points and one good one, Helen would focus on the good one—not just once, but every day.

Herbert E

My brother Herb, whom the family always called Herbert E, was one smooth, down-to-earth, hardworking person. I can never remember him not working at least a job and a half, if not two full-time jobs, at any time. And he caught on fast. If you showed him something one time and he asked a couple of questions, he had it. Although he only had a high school diploma, in my eyes he had a doctorate in science, mechanics, and social work.

He could fix anything. He had three sisters, and none of us had husbands. So when we needed something fixed around our homes or when our cars wouldn't run, we'd call Herbert E and he would fix it or get it running and it would stay running. What might cost you two hundred dollars to fix at a station, Herbert E would fix for six or seven dollars.

Later, when I moved to Ann Arbor, if anything broke, I'd say, "Put it on the list on the refrigerator. Herbert E will be here in May and he'll fix it."

He had hundreds of tools, and he knew where every one of them was. If a kid got something for Christmas that needed a tool to put it together, you could bet Herbert E had it in his truck, garage, or back room. If he had a job to do that he didn't know about—say, building a deck or a garage—he'd buy a book about it, read the book in a week, and lay out every tool and material he needed to start. Then he'd start working and not stop until he was finished.

He was also a motorcycle-lover. His bike was a Harley called the Pepper Shaker. I went to his house one day and he had it torn down. The two back rooms of his house that weren't used were covered with drop cloths, and on them he had every piece of that cycle. The largest part I could see was about the size of a grapefruit.

"What's wrong?" I asked.

"Nothing. I broke it down to clean it."

Herbert E started from the bottom on every job he had and before long he'd be running the place. He started off as an order picker in a warehouse in Cornwall Heights, Pennsylvania, and within a year, he was in charge of over sixty people in the warehouse. After another two years, he was in charge of all two hundred salesmen, and eventually he ended up running the place—learning computers and all the

ONE ROSE BLOOMING

electronic-age stuff that goes with big business.

"Isn't your boss afraid to let you do all that without a degree?" I asked.

"He's saving money," Herb said. "He'd have to pay somebody with the proper credentials $28 an hour. He pays me $8, plus $2 on the side, and I'm happy as a lark."

As hard as he worked for it, Herbert E wasn't generous with his money. He and I could agree on everything but that. If I saw someone who needed twenty bucks, I'd give it to him. Herbert E wouldn't give money. He wouldn't give you ten dollars, but he'd fix your house, rebuild your furnace, and put on a new roof.

Willie Simpson

I have never met any human being who could give someone the kind of encouragement Willie Simpson could. He was a student counselor at Washtenaw Community College for years and worked on getting grants for students. But Willie's real gift was going out and talking people into going back to school. Even people who had never considered going to college would fall under Willie's spell. He would talk to them, show them why they should go, and then he'd go and find financial support to make it happen.

Willie had a talent for getting young people to change their lives, elevate themselves so they could be independent of the welfare system. I think I'm good at this—real good. But I'm not as good as Willie was.

He could find hope in the hopeless. I hate to say it, but there were people I thought were just a lost cause that Willie would talk to like they were the future king and queen. He'd see someone stumbling down the street, higher than a Georgia pine, and say, "He's got beautiful teeth. Instead of drinking, he should be down at a magazine auditioning for a toothpaste ad."

Or he'd see a woman and say, "Come back to Washtenaw, get an education, and I bet you could model [or be in pictures...or write]." And it was always from the heart.

When he was dying of colon cancer—I think he was only forty-eight—he would still come to the hospital to spend time with my son Joe, who'd had his feet badly burned in an accident.

Being a black woman and being raised black, I love it when I meet black people who aren't racist. I really do. That was another thing I liked about Willie Simpson: He didn't have a racist bone in his body. And he was raised in the South at a time and place when he had every reason to hate white people. He judged every man individually on his behavior.

Willie Simpson didn't set a quota on helping people. Every time I saw him, he was encouraging people, working on getting them whole. That was one beautiful human being.

Those are my idols, my mentors. They are all gone now with the exception of Rich Ballard. But every so often I feel them there next to me—encouraging, pushing, challenging me to be a better person. It's good company I keep.

SEVENTEEN

The Day the Sky Fell In

CLOSE YOUR EYES AND IMAGINE for a moment how wonderful things would be for the human race if we could all be a bit more compassionate, a bit more sensitive, and a bit more understanding of each other. What holds us back from giving and caring? Especially when what's needed most is a sense of hope. That's all that is missing in most people's lives.

When there's hope among the downtrodden, the victimized, and the impoverished souls of this earth, great things can happen. Creative forces are let loose. The unimaginable is suddenly obtainable. I've seen it happen time after time.

And when people learn to give—to share some of themselves and their material wealth, sometimes until it hurts—they get hooked. Rather than sitting back and watching the world's woes mount, they are empowered to make things happen for the better.

On September 11, 2001, the sky fell in. After the tragedy of the terrorist attacks, Americans opened up their hearts and wallets as never before with an outpouring of prayers, money, and support for the families of the dead and wounded.

As helpful and reassuring as those acts of giving were, we can't let that generosity leave us contented and self-satisfied. Catastrophes happen every day in America and throughout the world. Children are hungry and malnourished. Families face economic ruin. Drugs destroy lives. Prejudice and bigotry snuff out hope and opportunity.

First, we need to recognize that we can't hide from these problems. Then we must do something to help. Americans learned after the tragedy of September 11 that there is such a great spiritual power in giving. Now we need to apply that lesson every day by rolling up our sleeves and pitching in to make someone's life just a bit easier. Prayers and good wishes are well and good, but we need to show compassion through our actions. If caring for each other becomes second nature to us—rather than a one-time, highly publicized event—future tragedies can be averted. Our sights should be set on preventing wars, not mopping up after them.

And we don't have to look far to find people who need our help. They are in all of our communities, neighborhoods, schools, and workplaces. They may be strangers, beggars, or the homeless, or they may be the children next door. They may even be those who live in ivory towers.

ONE ROSE BLOOMING

Our great challenge is to fulfill our earthly mission by being of service to one another. To do that, we must become better at disciplining ourselves spiritually. We all have it in us; we just need the willingness and the courage to change as individuals.

The effects of giving until it hurts—whether our gifts are financial or personal involvement—are far-reaching. We never know when and how our efforts will bear fruit, but bear fruit they will.

Please allow me just one more story. I'll make it short. It's about a kid named J. J. who was eleven years old when I first came to know him. He stayed in trouble all the time and didn't seem to be anyone's favorite—not even his parents'.

Over the years, J. J. acted out so badly that I was about to wash my hands of him. I didn't want to, but I told myself that in order to keep my sanity I had to. I had been dealing with him a long time, and nothing I did was working. I could tell J. J. loved me, but I couldn't reach him no matter what I did. I clothed him, fed him, and spent a great deal of time with him. I counseled him regularly. Nothing I did seemed to make a difference.

Then one day the principal called me to school for a meeting. I assumed it was about J. J.'s acting up again, and I showed up hesitantly, dreading the usual tale of how he was out of control.

When I arrived I saw a piece of paper with a list of names written in red ink on the principal's office door, and I said to myself, Oh, shit, they are about to throw J. J. out of school. I knew that would be it for him; he'd be lost for sure.

I opened the door and went into the principal's office. As I sat down tears began to well in my eyes as I waited for the bad news to be delivered.

"Ms. Martin, how did you feel, seeing our boy J. J.'s name among the list of honor roll students for the month?" the principal asked.

I nearly dropped my teeth in his water glass.

"What?" I said. "My J. J.?"

"Isn't it great," he said, " to see the results of all of us working together to help him learn?"

I am proud to say that our J. J. finished school, went to Eastern Michigan University, and graduated at the top of his class. He moved out of public housing and became an administrator at Johns Hopkins Hospital in Baltimore, Maryland. He's now working toward a master's degree in business administration.

I learned once again to pay attention to that voice inside me that accompanies that old boot kicking me in the butt—the voice that says, "Get agoin'. You have work to do."